LORAINE HAYNIE

CURSE

CONFRONTING THE PITCHFORD

Beverly Miller's Story of Love and Greed

As told to Loraine Haynie

Enjoy!

Beverly Pitchford Miller

ACKNOWLEDGEMENTS

First, I want to thank Beverly P. Miller for bringing her story to me. She offered intriguing hours of storytelling, long ago recorded tapes, family reference books, newspaper articles and internet web pages to detail her life events. She was upbeat, excited and always available when I had questions. She has a notable memory at 91 years of age and lived a remarkable life.

Next, I have to acknowledge and thank the Beta Readers who took hours of their time to edit, correct, suggest changes and overall promote a quality product from me. I was amazed at the lack of duplication in suggestions. Therefore, I feel the book has gotten an honest, thorough test of content and grammatical usage, allowing for some colloquialisms. I admire the folks who supported me through this process. It would not be the same level of quality if not for them. Love and praise for Mary Anderson, Brenda Austin, Barbara Collins, Linda

Martin, Linda Miller, Anita Scott, Betty Smith, Jane B. Smoot, Carol Stovall, Kathy VanLaar and Gloria Wilson.

I am blessed to have the above support group in my corner. They were my backbone and lifeline.

There are Demons within and
Demons without
The hardest to confront are
The Demons within

CONTENTS

CONFRONTING THE PITCHFORD CURSE

The doorbell's melodious chime causes a shrill barking from somewhere within the confines of the villa. In a few minutes, the face of a petite senior citizen pokes out the door. Upon seeing me, she widens the opening to reveal herself dressed in Chico's latest lavender and green floral jacket, anchored by forest green pants.

When I reach to shake her hand, I notice her nails groomed in a matching purple polish, her hair perfectly coiffed, and lavender dangling earrings darting in and out of her blonde shoulder –length hair. Beverly takes my hand, "Come in, dear. I'm so excited about our meeting. I've been gathering photos and newspaper articles to show you."

She closes the door and I follow her down the hall through her compact home, full of treasures left from downsizing three other homes to fit into the 1,400 square foot duplex villa in a fifty-five and older community. We walk in the opposite direction from the barking.

"Hush, Heidi," she commands. "She's in her crate. She won't bother us." As we sit in overstuffed chairs in the small den, she offers some of the pictures she pulled out of albums and she begins, "I hope you will find my story interesting and will want to write it. I promised my husband that I would tell our story before I die."

It is hard to imagine this soft-spoken grandmother as a powerhouse of real estate development, rubbing elbows with the elite in Washington, DC and engaging the money brokers in West Palm Beach, Florida. No one would expect a woman to negotiate million dollar deals in the 1970s and 80s.

Like her compact home, life is also more compact for Beverly. The days involve bridge and other card games at the clubhouse with neighbors. Shopping on-line for favorite deals from Chico's is a game for her, and having her hair and nails done helps her maintain an attractive appearance. She cooks for her family every Sunday, and enjoys reminiscing about her life. She is one of two Beverly Millers who live in the neighborhood, but her maiden name, Pitchford, clearly identifies her.

"I've had a wonderful life. I married my true love and we were still in love after 70 years together. My childhood provided me with adventure and fun and my family was the backbone of our community for years. I idolized my father and wanted to be just like him. I learned from him how to have a compelling career."

With a twinkle in her eye, she continues, "My father had five brothers. During the Great Depression, the family flourished in Jensen and Stuart, Florida, and had more than the average family. My dad was an entrepreneur and chose not to go to college. Four of his five brothers did go to college and had promising futures, but lurking in the background for the family was the "*Pitchford Curse*".

CHAPTER 1

The Spark of Jack

I met Lt. Bill Humphreys through friends in the summer of 1946 and we dated casually. He was a handsome, dark-haired man and we had fun together. We had several dates but our relationship wasn't serious. The Air Force deployed him to Morrison Field in West Palm Beach at that time, but scheduled to transfer him to California. On one date, we went to a wedding and reception for the Commanding Officer of the base and an Air Force nurse. An invitation to this event was a special honor for Bill and was the first time for me to be in the company of other officers at the base. I was impressed.

Later that summer, Bill invited me to a dance at the Officer's Club. We sat at a table with a crowd of his friends as the band began to play. I danced with Bill a few times and with a few of his friends, but with his back to me, it appeared that he was more interested in talking with old friends than dancing. That suited me.

I tapped my foot and swayed to the music, when a lieutenant came over to speak to one of the girls at our table and looked my way. Our eyes locked. After he looked at Bill, obviously busy visiting with friends, he slid over and asked me to dance.

I said, "I'd love to. My name is Beverly Ann."

As he escorted me to the dance floor, he responded, "I'm Jack Miller. My childhood sweetheart in Atlanta was named Beverly Ann." Before I realized it, we danced every dance the rest of the night. Our feet moved in tandem. We seemed to float on the dance floor. Our conversation came easy and we laughed as if we had known each other for years. We both realized that a little magic was going on between us, but the night ended without a commitment to see each other again.

Jack headed back to base operations at Morrison Field, and I headed back to Miami, where I lived with four other Pan American Stewardesses. I had a flight out the next day to Miami and Jack had a flight the next morning.

His handsome face burned in my mind and his easy-going manner intrigued me. He had an important job as an Air

Force Pilot. He was responsible for transporting some of the most powerful people in government, but he was not arrogant, distant, or condescending. He was funny, interesting and approachable. I wanted to get to know him, but my Pan Am flights took me out of the country with layovers for the next month.

Sometime later, in the fall when I got back to Miami, I flew up to West Palm Beach to see my mother and sister, Betty. At that time, I was working a shift of 15 days on and 15 days off. After my visit with them, it was time to head back to Miami. Waiting on a plane at the airport in West Palm Beach bored me. The control tower kept delaying the plane and I needed a distraction.

Therefore, I thought, "I'm going to call that Lieutenant that I danced with." I called over to the barracks and asked for Jack Miller. 'Lo and behold' he was there and answered the phone.

He immediately recognized my voice and said, "I'd like to see you."

I responded, "Come down to Miami, I'm living in Coral Gables now and we could meet at Dade's Drug Store."

He said, "What about Friday week after next?"

Trying hard to hide my excitement, I said, "That's fine. How about one o'clock?"

That is how we arranged our first date.

CHAPTER 2

Dade's Drug Store

Looking toward the glass door so I could see him approach, I positioned myself on the last stool at the soda fountain and wadded a napkin in my fist to absorb the sweat from my palms. I asked him to meet me at one o'clock to avoid the noon lunch crowd. As expected, there were only three other people at the counter. A man and woman with their backs to the door were not talking to each other, but looking at their watches every few minutes. The redheaded woman was dressed in a beige summer suit and had a briefcase on the floor at her feet. The man in a gray suit and tie also had a briefcase at his feet. They looked to be on their lunch hour, so I hoped they would leave in a few minutes. A teenage girl sat alone wearing a low-cut pink t-shirt and shorts, leaned over her Coke as she batted big brown eyes at the soda jerk, and toyed with her brown curly hair. She would not be a distraction to us.

The sun was high in the sky and cast shadows on the sidewalk through the palm trees. There was a cool path from the park across the street to the glass door at Dades. Pink hibiscus and yellow and pink lantana lined the sidewalk. Pedestrians lingered on the park benches across the street.

I looked in the mirror behind the lunch counter to double-check my reflection. My golden curls brushed my shoulders. My Florida-tanned face needed no makeup. I wore a blue silk blouse and long, gray, linen pants because they set-off my figure. They were appropriate for whatever we decided to do that day. Everything looked good.

The couple put money on the counter on top of their bill as they stood and simultaneously grabbed their brief cases and headed toward the door.

"Why in the world am I so nervous?" I thought. He seemed eager to see me again when I called him. Not sure why I did that. I felt sure he would show up. I just couldn't wait to see Jack. He said he knew where Dade's Drug Store was. He was right on time.

My heart beat rapidly as I watched him cross the street. Then he was there at the door with that big grin of his and everything *was* good. He was as handsome as I remembered in his Air Force khakis, starched and crisp. He removed his hat as he reached for the door. I got up and met him before he got inside. He smiled and took my hand and then pulled me into an embrace.

"Hi, beautiful," he said. The sun seemed to burst forth and light up the entire world around us. We moved over to the red stools at the lunch counter and his eyes swept over me with an approving look before he surveyed the drugstore.

"This is a neat place. I like the black and white tile floors and red trim around the white countertop. Ah ha, I see a juke-box. Want to dance?"

I was taking all of him in; giddy to be sitting beside him in a familiar place to me. It was my favorite place to lunch. "I don't think there is room to dance, but I'll try if you will."

"No, I'm starved. How about you?"

Surprisingly, I wasn't hungry. "I can always eat a bite or two."

We ordered sandwiches and lemonade and talked a little there at the drug store while we ate our lunch. I barely touched mine but Jack didn't seem to notice.

As we finished our lunch, Jack said, "Let's get out of here and go over to Miami Beach and go clubbing."

I was fine with that. Rising from the stools, his hand slid down my arm and laced my fingers as we walked to his Garnet Maroon 1940 Ford convertible parked at the curb in front of the park. My hand and arm were still tingling when he opened the car door for me. I smiled up at him, wondering what the night would hold.

We went to several clubs in Miami, danced and had a few cocktails. My life as a stewardess had introduced me to casual drinking, which was something new for me. Later, Jack said he needed some fresh air, so we went outside.

"The dancing was fun and I loved holding you in my arms, but we haven't been able to talk. Let's go for a walk." Once again, he took my hand and the pure pleasure of his touch made my head spin.

"You're beautiful, are a great dancer, have a great smile and are easy to be with, but I want to know more about who you are."

I needed no other nudge; "I am a native Floridian, born in Jensen Beach. I have worked for Pan American as a stewardess for about a year. It is an exciting job and I get to see many places I would never see otherwise. My mom and sister live in West Palm Beach and I visit with them when I'm not flying. How about you?"

Without letting go of my hand, he motioned for us to sit on a wooden park bench under the glow of a dimmed street lamp, "I'm not a Floridian. I was born and educated in Atlanta. I always loved planes and flying, so I joined the Air Force and I am stationed at Morrison Field. I'm planning to be a career pilot."

We had such a good time walking, talking, and getting to know each other. The weather was perfect for this kind of date.

Before I realized it, the evening was getting late, so we headed back to Jack's car. Driving toward Coral Gables on the causeway, we drove into in a typical Florida deluge. Jack drove carefully, but the car hydroplaned and slid off the road. When we came to a stop, the car tilted a little to my side leaning off a small bank. Jack threw his door open and bounded over to my side of the car.

He jerked the door open and helped me step out of the car onto sand and slippery grass. "Are you okay?" he asked with a shaky voice

I tried to sound calm. "I'm fine. " I said, looking down at the hem of my favorite pair of pants. They were now wet with grass stains and sand soaking into the delicate linen fabric. The rain had stopped, but my pants took the punishment.

I was nervous about how we would get home, and get the car to a repair shop. However, almost immediately, the police arrived. I do not know how they knew about the accident, but I was afraid they would smell alcohol on our breaths and take us to jail.

The police got us off the road and offered us a ride to the police station so Jack could call friends to come get us. His friends from the base were in town on a weekend leave and they came with much teasing and joking and picked us up at the police station.

They took me back to the house where I was staying on Anastasia Boulevard in Coral Gables. Jack apologized profusely on the way. At my front door, he leaned in, gave me a kiss on the forehead, and said, "I had a great time!"

"Me too." I smiled up at him. When he walked away, he looked back at me a couple of times. As he got back in the car with his friends, he waved and offered his compelling smile. Then they left.

That was a memorable first date!

I am not sure if the way I met Jack was fate or destiny. It happened like so many things I began to see in my life. I was in the right place at the right time, but if everything had not lined up exactly right; I could have missed the opportunity to meet him. If Bill had not invited me to the dance, if I had been on a flight that weekend, or if Bill had danced with me when Jack came over to the table, I would have never met Jack. Was it fate or was a higher power leading me?

CHAPTER 3

Building on Our Relationship

I saw Jack a couple of weeks later while in West Palm Beach visiting my mother. We had a short date that time because I had a flight trip the next day.

I had my mother's car and picked him up in front of base operations. "It's so good to see you," he said as he opened the passenger seat door. His eyes sparkled when he smiled at me. We sat in the car a moment just looking at each other. The air inside wrapped me with his presence. When I could pull my eyes away from him, I suggested that we go to Werts, my favorite place in Palm Beach. It was a fun place to go and right on Ocean Avenue, in the center of everything; but we could have been anywhere.

Most of our conversation that day included airplanes. "I love flying. I never dreamed that I would love the flying part of this job, especially during take-off when the plane defies gravity and lifts you into the heavens. I knew I would love the places where my flights would take me, but I had no idea that I would love being in the air, above the clouds, experiencing the feeling that I belonged there."

Jack's eyes lit up as he took my hand, "I feel the same way. Flying is ethereal. I have loved planes since I was a little boy, but when I actually got inside the plane and held the instruments, I knew this was my life. I had to fly."

We had a connection the moment we met, and this love of flying strengthened that connection. The afternoon was way too short. I dropped him off at the base and headed home.

While I was in West Palm Beach, my roommate, Betty, met up with Nelle Hardy and some of the other flight attendants. They hatched a plan for the five of us to live together in Miami Beach.

Betty called me, "I've been taking with Nelle and some other stewardesses. With fall just around the corner, wouldn't it be fun to live on Miami Beach? We would enjoy the beach life and party when we're on our days off from work, especially when we're on short trips and don't have time to go anywhere away from home base."

That sounded good to me. "Sure. But where can we find a place we can afford?"

"If five of us go in together, we can find an affordable place. Are you in if we find the perfect place?"

"Sure. Count me in." I couldn't let an opportunity like that pass me by.

They decided on the Coral Reef Hotel and reserved a suite that could accommodate us. Before I arrived back in Miami, Betty moved my things into the suite that had only two bedrooms and four beds. The five of us managed with only four beds because the rotation scheduled one of us on a trip all the time. Therefore, we had enough beds and the suite was a perfect solution.

The small Coral Reef Hotel on 36 and Collins had a swimming pool. We had so many good times there and partied on our short leaves. Pan Am made sure that we had excellent accommodations wherever we had to stay. They even had a maid that came in each morning and opened the curtains for us. My roommates who did not have a steady boyfriend were out a lot, but the two that did have boyfriends had them over regularly. Men filled the crowded rooms regularly. When the guys finally left, the 'girls' could visit and talk about our whirlwind life. I did confide in Nelle and another stewardess about my feelings for Jack, but I could not tell them about my fears, hopes, dreams and family.

After I moved to the Coral Reef, Jack called and said he wanted to see me. He came to Miami to check on his car repair from the time we slid off the causeway. I learned that he would always be unpredictable, like me.

He showed up in a jitney (taxicab) and said. "I want you to go somewhere with me." Therefore, we took the jitney over to Coral Gables and went to the paint and body shop, repairing the car.

He told the owner, "I want you to paint the car blue, the color of her eyes."

How romantic can you get? Jack did so many unexpected special things for me over the years.

Jack came down there constantly and we all enjoyed him. Nelle Hardy was from Atlanta, too; she and Jack had so much fun entertaining us with singing old Atlanta songs. In the beginning, it was one big party. He worked at base operations at Morrison Field in West Palm Beach, so the guys up there asked him why he came to Miami so often.

Always the jokester, he told them, "I've got a harem down in Miami."

When we heard this story, five of us got on an airplane, flew up to West Palm Beach from Miami, and went to the base. I called Jack to tell him the plan so he could be on the lookout for us. When he saw us, he immediately came across the field in a military Jeep. We all squeezed on the Jeep and went over to base operations. When the men saw us their eyes lit up like Christmas trees.

Jack said, "Here is my harem." We carried on over him to complete the deception. He became a very popular man after that.

When tourist season started and hotel rates increased, we could not afford to stay on Miami Beach on our stewardess pay, so we moved back to Miami. We found a little three-room house on 50th street. The shotgun house was located behind the luxurious home of the woman who rented to us. It had one bedroom, another room that held two couches and a daybed and a tiny kitchen and bath. We had to sleep four. It was a huge letdown from the Coral Reef Hotel, but I had gotten tired of the constant parties and their intrusion into my home life. I needed some time to rest after the long trips traveling for so many days.

In those days, Pan Am scheduled me two weeks on and two weeks off and then the following rotation one week on and one week off. Flight rules limited our time in the air, so I spent almost as many days up in West Palm as I did in Miami. While in West Palm Beach, I explored the city. One day, I noticed several signs that said 'Kennedy Compound.' As I followed the signs, the last one near the police station cautioned, "Gentiles Only". I got a good laugh out of that.

Our schedules allowed us to see each other often. We frequently rented a bicycle with a basket seat and a driver who peddled us around the city. I showed Jack the sign and we laughed at that sign each visit. Cultures change.

By then Jack had met my mom. He and Mom hit it off immediately and he made himself at home at Mom's house. Jack and I went up and down the road between West Palm Beach and Miami many times in that little blue convertible.

Jack showed up there every time I came home. I wanted to see him, but he did some things that aggravated me. Occasionally I just wanted to visit with Mom. One time he bought me a bathing suit, and Mom thought he made a sweet gesture. I put it on and it fit perfectly. The blue color matched my eyes and it wasn't too revealing. That called for a picnic.

We packed a basket, went to the beach, swam in the ocean and had a lot of fun, even though I had been a little upset with him. (What man buys woman a bathing suit?)

Then another time, another holiday, he bought me a jump suit that fit me perfectly. A boy never bought me anything like that before. Jack was different. I could not get upset, because love had smitten me. Christmas, he left me the following card:

"Dearest,
Merry Xmas. May I spend the rest of my life
With the sweetest girl in the entire world.
All my love,
Your Jack"

CHAPTER 4

My Beginning

Little did Jack know that he had fallen in love with a woman whose family history was so much more complicated than his Atlanta family. At that time, I didn't understand the grip my dad's family would hold over my life. I had not learned about the "curse" or experienced its devastation. It would be many years before I understood fully how it would affect my career and me. I told Jack what I knew about my family at that time.

One weekend when we were at Mom's house in West Palm Beach, we both had experienced a busy week and wanted to laze around doing nothing. Mom worked at a local jewelry store since she and Dad divorced, and she had to work that Saturday, so we had the house to ourselves. As we drank a beer on the back patio, I began to tell Jack my story.

"I'm told that my dad wanted a boy. However, he got me, his first-born. Mom said I was a skin on bones, bald-headed girl. Dad accepted the situation and made the best of it, like most people during the Depression. Times were hard during those years for most of the country. Gratitude girded families. They made the best of what they had. Disappointment was not in their thought process. Therefore, Dad made the best of me.

As I grew, he took me fishing, hunting and showed me how to build things. He instilled in me an attitude that I could do anything. He never coddled or blamed. "

Mom loved to tell the story about the night I was born, which was a cold December 17, 1927. In spite of the weather, Dad wanted to go fishing, and since Mom was due to deliver me in a couple of weeks, he would not leave her at home alone. Mom was enjoying the starlit sky out in the rowboat, on the Indian River in Florida. Dad wasn't a romantic guy. His eyes were not on the stars; they scanned the rippled water. He spied a better fishing spot behind Mom, so he decided to swap places with her to get to where the fish were popping the top of the water. She shimmied over to give him room, but he tripped on something in the bottom of the boat and fell over on her, knocking her flat on her back into the floor of the boat. That started her contractions. In a panic, they rushed to the dock, tied up the boat and set out for the hospital in Fort Pierce, Florida. By the time they arrived, labor was imminent for Mom; there was no time to administer anesthesia. Dad said that my birth was very painful, but he sat beside Mom the entire time, holding her hand. Then, finally, he was the first to hold me.

That unconventional start to life was typical of my childhood—unpredictable, dramatic and memorable. Over time, Jack learned the rest of the story.

Dad was a creative, entrepreneurial force that knew how to charm people and make money. He was generous and giving. He shared what we had with the people in our community without hesitation. If he saw someone in need, he found a way to help him or her out. I spent my childhood learning everything from him and adored him. I wanted to be just like him, until I realized that he was not always the man I admired. He wanted to make money from his creative endeavors, which were sometimes on the edge of legal or ethical. That desire took him places I never wanted to go.

My father's name is William Weymss Pitchford, born to Joseph (Joe) and Kate Agnes Pitchford. He was the oldest of six sons. His Mother, Kate Weymss, whose prominent family migrated from Scotland to North Carolina, married Joseph Pitchford. The Civil War had left North Carolina with many hardships in the late 1800's. Joe had been born in Sewalls Point, Florida near Jensen Beach, so he and Kate moved to Jensen Beach from Warrenton, NC.

The Pitchford family were early settlers and founding fathers. The family appears in many of the history books of south Florida, but times were hard. Grandfather Pitchford worked on the railroad along with his brothers, Blount and Thomas. Life, at that time, wasn't prosperous like the Plantation era had been.

Early on, the 156-mile Indian River linked Volusia County and Palm Beach County as the main mode of transporting goods. Later, the Flagler Railroad extended its lines into West Palm Beach. Thomas was the first Pitchford to venture into the new territory down in Florida. The Pitchford drive was evident throughout the family. Thomas farmed in Dade County where the Miami Courthouse now stands.

Blount and, Joseph landed in Jensen Beach, 90 miles north of Dade County. Pineapple farms were flourishing in the late 1800's. The Pitchford brothers acquired 400 acres of prime waterfront property for pineapple farming. Three of their farms were beachfront. Many black laborers moved from Georgia, North Carolina and the Bahamas to work the farms.

The Pitchford family brought many of their old Southern traditions to their new lands. They owned the local water company, and tourist cottages. Grandfather was the Market Agent for other farmers in the area and shipped beans and other crops to the New York market by rail.

It was a time of plenty. The Pitchford family became the movers and shakers in the region. They were creative and industrious. They worked hard and accrued wealth like many other families in the area.

Grandfather Pitchford built a mansion on a five-acre parcel next to the Indian River. It had five bedrooms and Grandmother named it the "Periwinkle". The second house on the property became home to "Uncle" Abe and "Aunt" Renna, a black couple who were from Georgia. Abe helped maintain the property and Renna was the housekeeper; she also cooked and served the meals in the big house and bossed the boys when they needed it. Abe and Renna adored the Pitchford family.

When I was only four years old, I noticed how neat Renna kept their cabin, even though she cleaned the Periwinkle, too. Her energy made an impression on me, even as a four-year old.

"Aunt Renna, why do you scrub the wood floors with that lye soap until they change to white?"

"Baby girl, I want my floors to shine. I love clean. That's why I love cleaning the Periwinkle. It is such a beautiful home. I couldn't abide it if was dirty."

Uncle Abe had the same work ethic as Aunt Renna. Our family had pet monkeys, named Johnnie and Mary who lived in a cage. Abe fed the monkeys and walked them in the monkey cage.

"Uncle Abe. Why do you walk Johnnie and Mary in their cage? That is silly. They can walk outside on a leash."

"Oh, no, Miss Bev. They can't be trusted out of the cage. They would break loose and run free. I'd never be able to catch them."

As my parents were settling in as a couple, Grandmother Kate Pitchford was a big part of their everyday life. She welcomed Mom into the family with open heart and arms. She was delighted to have another female in her family. It was not always easy to be around men all the time. Mom told me about her first real conversation with Grandmother Pitchford after she and Dad married.

"Wanda, I'm so happy to have another woman to talk with. Men know nothing about decorating and entertaining and don't appreciate my efforts to make our home a warm and welcoming place for them and for company to visit."

"Mother Pitchford, I appreciate all you are teaching me with your organization skills. I am fortunate to have you as an example."

Mom shared many conversations she had with Grandmother Pitchford.

Grandfather Pitchford was free to concentrate on business and growing their fortune because Grandmother Kate handled everything else.

Grandmother Kate and Grandfather Joe were enjoying the boom time in Florida. They purchased properties along Florida's East coast and over to Orlando. They co-owned the first Orange County hotel. Grandmother loved entertaining and hosted guests in grand style. She inherited her mother's china, silver and linens and set an enviable table with little effort. She was an Eastern Star and participated in other women's groups.

The family also owned Pitchford's Camp, which Uncle Blount developed. It contained 30 cottages, trailer spaces, apartments, a restaurant, a grocery store and a bait and tackle shop, which had a 200-foot pier and a gas station with an upstairs apartment. Uncle Blount developed it as well as Pitchford Subdivision. That property, combined with Grandfather Joe's 200 acres west of the camp, gave the family a considerable portion of Jensen Beach.

When it was completed, the camp was in a premiere location for vacationers. The tightly packed dirt roads throughout the camp moved traffic without incident. Most local streets were dirt in those days. The apartments were popular rentals, because they were on the river and in close proximity to all the entertainment and businesses. The Indian River beckoned anglers with the promise of a fruitful catch. Steps away from the camp, the Jensen Bridge spilled sunbathers onto the beach at the Atlantic Ocean. Some guests came explicitly for the fishing, ate at the restaurant and bought their groceries from the store.

When Grandmother passed away I was only three months old, but I heard wonderful stories about her and the talent she had for entertaining. There was always an event going on at the Big House.

On her death, everything changed for the Pitchford men, especially Grandfather. He knew how to be a successful businessman. He was an upstanding townsman (mayor and a County Commissioner for a while), and he was an inspiring Sunday School Superintendent at the Congregational Church. I never saw him without a suit and tie on, but I thought he was a little on the snobby side, a little pompous.

It had been easy for him to ignore his sons. He did not know how to be a father. He relied on Grandmother to take care of their school and social education. He had never guided his sons in spiritual, ethical or educational ways. He neglected showing them how to be members of society. They did not know how to take care of their money, their property or their lives. He could not pass on his values, work ethic or responsibilities for taking care of themselves. He appeared lost without Grandmother and his brother.

As they grew older, that lack of parental training was evident. However, four of the six sons went to college. My dad, Bill, had always been an innovator and continued that role. That was his style. He was an extraordinary man: smart, talented, energetic and smooth taking. He never met a stranger and was generous. Dad married my mom and stayed in Jensen Beach, and after college, the other sons went their separate ways.

Joe left to work on a ship as a hydrographer for about eight years. Tom, who had been a scholar, slowly lost his mind. From an accident at Georgia Southern College, Herb had a plate in his head. He was coddled the rest of his life and was eventually called the "armchair traveler". Doc latched on to my dad and wanted what Dad had. Allan was only fourteen and had no guidance until he joined the Navy.

After his service in the Navy, Allan married his high school sweetheart and ran Bill's Place for my dad for a few years. He started Stuart Bridge Tender, which was a lucrative business. The bridge tender operated drawbridges to permit marine passage on inland waterways, near shores, and at danger points in waterway passages. The Jensen drawbridge on the Indian River opened and closed dozens of times each day to allow cargo ships and pleasure boats to pass through it. It was an interesting and active job.

In some cases, life went on in a normal sort of way. Grandfather Pitchford continued having the annual Christmas dinner. My mom, Aunt Carrie and other women visiting from the Carolinas prepared the house for celebrating and did all the cooking. One of my first memories of the Big House Homestead, "Periwinkle", was when I was about five years old.

It was a two-story house with a large front yard about 200 feet on the Indian River. The boys sometimes played ball games on the carpet-like lawn. Lilacs and other blooming plants grew along the front wall, which separated the house from the river. Mom and Aunt Carrie tried to keep up Grandmother's level of society and social graces, but it was impossible. It was Grandmother's home, and even though her spirit remained, the culture and sophistication were gone. It was a man's place now.

One Christmas, I joined all the men in their annual shooting contest. Dad liked to include me in competitions. They were shooting at targets nailed to posts out in the river.

"Dad, can I watch you shoot at the targets?"

He was quick to respond. "Of course, Bev, but I think you should try your hand at shooting."

I was excited about that offer.

When it was my turn, Dad bragged, "Now you boys better watch out. Don't let Beverly show you up." They all laughed at his joke.

His comment didn't bother me. I slowly raised the rifle, propped my arm on the fencing, squeezed the trigger and hit the bullseye dead center. Of course, it was purely an accident, but Dad claimed that he was training me to shoot black bears on the Hutchinson Island, which was across the Indian River.

Grandfather's sister, Carrie, spent most winters at Periwinkle. In addition, Grandfather's brother, Blount, who never married, lived with the family until he died.

I grew up with this family and my mom's family in Jensen Beach, Florida, which was the best place to spend a childhood. There were rivers, beaches, close-knit neighbors, friends and family. There were adventures almost every day.

My mother, Wanda Madelyn Lyons, was born in Virden, Illinois, on December 19, 1907. Her family moved to Springfield, when she was 17. That is where she and her younger brother, Britten (Britt), spent their adolescent years. They lived near their extended family of aunts, uncles and grandparents. She won the Miss Springfield, Illinois contest as a junior in high school, and began a career as a shoe model.

Mother was beautiful and smart, but the cold winters caused her to have many health problems. She suffered greatly in the winter months, so Britt encouraged their family to move to Vero Beach. After she graduated, the family did move to Florida. Grandma Lyons contacted her friend, Mrs. Higby, who owned and managed the restaurant on the Pitchford's property. (It became Dina's Café.) Mrs. Higby was instrumental in helping my grandparents settle in Jensen Beach.

Grandma, Zola Mae Lyons, came from a very aristocratic family. My grandpa was talented in many ways, but in his early years, worked as a conductor at the Illinois Century Railroad.

On Memorial Day, Dad went to Vero Beach to visit friends and they went to a baseball game and then to the beach. As the story goes, Dad's friend saw Grandma and Mom walking down the beach.

Dad said that his friend tapped him on the shoulder and pointed across the beach, "Hey, Bill, I see some folks I know. Let's go over and speak with them."

The friends introduced Grandma and Mom to Dad. My dad said, "I was smitten by your Mom at first sight, and thought she was the most beautiful girl I'd ever seen. Her dark hair, sparkling eyes and sweet smile pulled at my heartstrings."

Dad was a persuasive, handsome man and wanted to assure that he could see Mom again. During the course of the day, he convinced Grandma to move to Jensen Beach so she could be closer to her friend, Mrs. Higby. His friend told him Grandma had left all her friends in Illinois and was lonely.

Dad ran the gas station on the Indian River. There was an apartment over the filling station that was vacant. Dad convinced Grandma that the family could stay in the apartment until they found a better place to live. It was in the middle of everything in Jensen, and it provided conveniences for them while they learned the town. It was close to their friends, so it was an easy sell for him to make.

Every time Mom came down the stairs from the apartment, she almost ran into my dad's arms. It had not taken long for their attraction to grow. He was always at the station, hanging around the stairs, waiting to see her. She would stop and they would talk or walk around the camp. It was obvious that they were in love.

Mom said that my grandparents became a little worried at the attention my dad was giving her. It appeared to be a blooming romance.

However, Grandma said, "This is a passing fancy. It won't last long."

It just so happened that my mother heard that remark and immediately told my dad. Dad said, "Well, we'll fix that! We'll elope." Mom agreed and they began making plans for their elopement.

Mom told Grandma, "Bill and I are going to see the orange groves in Vero Beach". She had earlier slipped a little overnight bag down to my dad in the gas station.

They did go to Vero Beach, but they did not see the orange groves; instead, they married and spent their honeymoon in Melbourne, Florida.

Mom and Dad moved into the Big House on Grandfather Pitchford's estate in the room my father had as a boy. Later, they moved into a house on the estate on Church Street, right behind the Big House. Uncle Blount was instrumental in developing the Pitchford Subdivision (Blount's Subdivision). He gave Lot

6 to Mom and Dad as a wedding gift, and after a few months, they built a house there. It was at the end of the Jensen Bridge, about a mile north of the big house. That is where they settled down and where I spent my childhood until age twelve.

I had many memories growing up around that Jensen Bridge. I went down on the docks with my dad and caught little fish, and sometimes rode my bike. When I was five years old, I rode my bike off the end of the dock into the water and Dad rescued me.

Later during WWII, the Navy had a small house built on the bridge for airplane spotters. I received a license from the Fort Pierce Coast Guard to be one of the spotters. Many things happened down on the bridge during wartime. At night, all the houses had their lights off or had heavy drapes over the windows. We had big blinds and kept the lights out at night. Submarines from Germany were very close to the shoreline, and they sank a big ship not too far south of where we were. One morning Dad went out into the ocean to fish at the inlet and spotted a submarine. He immediately called the authorities. He received a Commendation for notifying the Navy about the submarine.

Dad was always fooling around with wild animals. One time he brought a baby skunk home, and as we gathered around it in awe, he said, "I've had it de-skunked; that way we can keep it for a pet".

The first time the skunk got a little upset and put out a 'bark', all the kids ran, holding our noses, "Daddy, come get this skunk; he's smelled up the whole house!" They had a terrible time getting rid of that smell! He taught me to appreciate all life the way he did. He even built a little mice house, where he raised white mice that he sold for research.

However, the most engaging creatures he brought me from his fishing trips were little birds. On those days, I squatted near the house so I wouldn't scare the birds and waited for his return. He put them in a washtub with a screen on top. When he was ready, I crept down to the water and caught elusive sand fleas in the seaweed to feed the birds. For a few days, I was the one in charge of those birds. I loved being in charge and watching them open their beaks to let me feed them. I loved all creatures in that water wonderland.

I also buried turtle eggs under the kitchen window to protect them. I checked every day for them to hatch and when they finally did, I watched them purposefully 'sand paddle' to the sea. Dad provided me with a full education of nature.

Other things interested me too. Entertainment was everywhere. I made my rounds daily. The train tracks ran through the edge of our property. One of my favorite activities of the day was to trek through the woods, and hike up the hill to the railroad tracks where I chose a spot on a large rock to wait for the trains to slow down, but not stop, and snatch the mailbags. I was amazed that they never missed.

I also spent hours watching the Bridge Tender walk around and around the bridge. He held a long metal pipe to open the drawbridge, letting the ships go through. I got excited when sometimes the ships would back up waiting for the drawbridge to open. I sat there and dreamed of where each ship had been and where it might be going. I imagined life in faraway places.

I had a friend, Margaret Snipes, whose family lived in a house on the bridge. I spent the night with her one time.

"Margaret, it's so exciting to know that there is all kinds of water-life under us, swimming, or fighting over a meal. In a way it's creepy."

"You get used to it." Shrugging her shoulders, she fell asleep quickly. However, sleep didn't come easy for me that night. I listened to the sounds of the water life, the breaking of waves against the pier and the quiet of the rest of the world. It was both scary and beautiful.

My family owned the property on both sides of the road to the beach, which was about 225 acres. There was a canal along beach road called "the ditch". Dad kept several boats in the ditch. A homeless man lived in one of the abandoned boats.

In my child's mind, I imagined the homeless man skulking around the area at night. He looked for food and collected discarded items to put in the boat to make it more comfortable. When I saw him at a distance, I ran the other way. I wondered how he could live like that—no bathroom, no stove, and no bed. I wondered how he became homeless, even though there were few jobs available during the Depression. I wondered how he spent his time each day. He made a big impact on me. I decided right then I would never be homeless. I knew, along with Dad's training, I would work hard and make sure that did not happen to me.

Many creatures were part of my life during those years. We had tailless black cats; Dad cut their tails cut off so we could tell them from our neighbor's black cats. I had a calf named Libby that I raised from a baby when the mother died. An owl lived in a rope on the back porch. I loved my first dog, Bow, who chased cars. One day as we walked to Grandfather's house, a trailer hit and killed him. I found a baby squirrel and kept it

29

in a shoebox by the fireplace until she got out and burned in the fire. Dad even brought home a baby alligator that I kept until mom evicted it.

The Segerstroms were our Swedish friends. They moved across from Mom and Dad on Church Street. Mom taught Edith to speak English, and the hours they spent together ensured they would become close friends. Mr. Segerstrom raised pineapples like Grandfather Pitchford. They were friends from the beginning.

Their daughter, Connie, was a year older than I was and she became my very first "best friend". We had a lot of fun doing the simple things of life. We spent many hours in rowboats going the two-mile stretch from her house to mine. We made spears that we used to spear stingrays and other water life.

When I was a little girl about five or six years old, I got my first boat. Connie and I paddled around the Indian River in that little washtub boat. Of course, the adults chaperoned us. Later we had a scow, which was a bigger boat. We used to pull it by placing our oars on the bottom of the river. We used all our strength, to force the boat forward, as we went up and down the river catching fish.

We found or created an adventure daily. The train that went through Jensen in those days burned coal. I can still picture the red-hot flicker of fire sparking under the trains, and I still hear the metal on metal wheels as they roar by. Every day I looked for the sparks to ignite the dry brush. As a barefoot child, I joined the other family members, cutting palm fronds and beating the fires out. They were small fires, but they could have gotten bigger if we had not put them out. What was an adventure for me, turned into an emergency effort for the community. These inspiring, invigorating experiences set the tone for me for the rest of my life.

One of my dad's enterprises was a small cow shed where he kept a couple of cows on the back of our property. We also had beehives on the side of the shed. We had plenty of fresh honey. Dad did things the unique way. I can remember, he also had a beehive on the side of the garage. He could see it through the glass window while he was working. He milked his cows and shared the fresh milk with everybody in Jensen. Those were the days of the Depression, so times were not so good. Everybody was poor, but we didn't know it. We had plenty to eat because of Dad's garden, cows, fish and milk.

Connie's mother often told the story about the time we were coming to her house to visit. She said, "Oh, I'd invite you to dinner, but I don't have anything to cook."

My Dad said, "Wait a minute." He went out and in a little while, he came back with fresh rabbits. They cooked the rabbits and they had dinner that night. This was the thoughtful man my dad was.

Raising cattle was a lot of fun. One of the cows did not accept her calf. Dad said, "He didn't make it. He has passed on. He's dead." Therefore, he asked Slim, one of the workers there, to dig a hole for burial. As Slim was getting ready to dig, my mother said, "Oh, I saw him move. He's not dead." Therefore, she decided to nurse him back to health using Libby's canned milk. That is how Libby became my little calf; she trailed behind me like a puppy dog.

Mom and Dad's monkeys needed fresh produce to eat. One day Dad had gone to Stuart to deliver water from Jensen Pure Water, the bottling company they owned, and Mom had gone to get the produce that a store saved for the monkeys. When Dad saw Mom coming up the road, he stopped in the middle of the railroad tracks without thinking. He flagged her down as she approached his water truck.

Mom told me that he was so excited that he could not wait to tell her, "Wanda I've bought a bunch of carrots for you. Since you walked into a tree in the dark the other night, I've been worried about you and I heard that carrots are good for night-blindness." He was very thoughtful like that. His concern surprised Mom, but she smiled and thanked him.

Another one of my early memories was when my dad killed the last bear ever shot on the Barrier Hutchinson Island. Earlier, my grandfather had killed the largest bear ever shot on the island. As long as I can remember that bear skin hung on the wall at the entrance of the Big House. My grandfather shot the biggest bear and my father shot the last bear. However, Dad's bear was not so small either.

Dad was an early riser; he always said he would have his work done before half the people were out of bed. He could not remember not seeing the sunrise. He used to go over to the island on what they called rut roads before there were any paved roads. The only building on the island was about five miles south of the inland and was a house of refuge, where immigrants would temporarily live. Between Jensen Beach Bridge and the house of refuge, there were about five miles of rut roads where farms were located on the island.

Sometimes, Dad would ask, "Would you go rabbit hunting with me in the morning?" I jumped up early, dressed in pants and a loose shirt and ran to the car to steer it. I looked for every opportunity to be with Dad. My skinny legs hung loosely above the floor, but that was okay because my job was to steer the car and keep it in the ruts. While I worked the steering wheel, Dad sat outside on the fender with a straw hat hiding his face. He never looked at me as he aimed downward, shooting rabbits, and we never came back empty handed. He was a very good shot.

During the first 12 years of my life, the Indian River was my playground. The water and canopy of trees offered limitless hours of exploration in the nooks and crannies full of delightful creatures, which I believed God placed them there for my fun and pleasure. I had no concept of its size. I did not know it was over five miles wide in places and only four feet deep, that it was only one of three lagoons, or that it spanned from Ponce de Leon Inlet to Jupiter Inlet in Palm Beach County. I was in or on it every day but didn't know or care about these facts.

Our cousins lived next door. The oldest were twins, Louis and Lawrence; the others were Blount, Dick and Joyce. Joyce was my age and we had many adventures together.

Louis and Lawrence built a barge from cross ties discarded by the railroad. One day Joyce and I noticed the barge tied on the shore of the river. "Hey Joyce, what is that tied up on the shore?"

"It's a barge my brothers built. It's not really useful for anything."

"Are you kiddin'? We could have a great adventure floating down the river. It's large enough that we could stretch out and sun bathe," I prodded.

She looked over the barge with a new interest and yielded, "Okay, let's take her out."

We poled out into the river. When we reached the channel, the current jerked the pole away from us, leaving us helpless. The current was taking us toward Fort Pierce, and we drifted over two miles before someone saw us and towed us back home. I avoided the cousins, Louis and Lawrence, for a little while after that to distance myself from their anger.

The first major change in my life happened on November 19, 1931, when my sister, Betty Jean, was born. There were so many years between us that we just did not get close. I was busy with my explorations and did not have a desire to spend time with a baby who distracted my parents from me. Grandma and Grandpa Lyons were living in the same apartment over the store on the riverfront. I was jealous of Betty because Grandma Lyons seemed to be rocking her all the time.

"Grandma, why don't you come outside and watch me play?" I would encourage.

"Betty needs her bottle and a good burping and then I'll put her down, but I need to straighten the house when I get through. You have Joyce to play with."

I loved Grandma, but I would get so mad that she never seemed to have time for me anymore. When I got an opportunity, I would sneak up behind Grandma and pinch her arm while she held Betty. She never scolded me for that or told Mom about it.

As the years went by, I grew more jealous of Betty and the time she spent with Grandma and Mom. She seemed to need so much, but I needed them, too. They did not think about that.

Joyce and I continued with our adventures. I was happy outside, but wished Mom would come out and spend time with me, rather than staying inside when she was not at work.

Joyce and I built a platform at the water's edge where we ate our sandwich lunches each day. One day, when she was about three years old, Betty, saw us eating our lunch on the platform and ran down to the river with our dog Bow to be with us. When Bow saw me, he ran out into the river, leaped on the platform and flipped it over, tossing us into the river.

I screamed at Betty, "When you bring Bow outside, you need to watch him and be more careful. Look what you've done." I began righting the platform with Joyce as Betty ran home to Mom, crying. We recovered and righted the platform. However, when I went inside, to change clothes, Mom fussed at me for being mean to Betty. I felt that Mom always blamed me for something I did to Betty. She just could not fit into my world.

I was not that interested in school. I always wanted to be doing something to make money. It was just my nature *and* from watching my dad. It started when I was five or six years old. Dad taught me how to catch baitfish. I dug worms on the shore and put them in a pail, and then I sat on the dock and caught grunts. The grunts were about the same size as sailor bait, but the sailor bait was not good for catching fish because they had sharp fins.

There was a 200- foot pier in front of our house, which was a popular place for fishing. One day as I watched the number of anglers grow larger all day, I realized that these men needed bait to catch fish. I enjoyed fishing too, so I sat on the dock and began catching grunts and placing them in a bucket. When I had enough grunts in my bucket, I would walk down the bridge to the pier and sell them for bait to the fishermen. I charged $.05 for each cup of grunts. With the money I made, I would go over to our grocery store and buy a penny's worth of candy.

When my dad saw what I was doing, he praised my entrepreneurship. In addition, he gave me his old fishnets to use so I could catch more fish.

Joyce and I set the nets out and the next morning they overflowed with fish. However, the fish were gar. They were not good for eating. That ended my first big enterprise in business, but I got a picture of our catch put in the local paper.

This was my first attempt in the world of business. Even though it was a failure, it got my juices flowing and fired up my interest in making an idea grow and be profitable. In addition, I learned to work. I worked at something all my life. I cannot remember a time in my life when I was not working.

Grandfather Joe, Uncle Blount and Uncle Thomas set a high bar for achievement. They built a fortune using all this country has to offer to build a wonderful life. Their belief in hard work and achievement encapsulated me. I recognized my difference with Dad's brothers. I saw them lazing around. They were nothing like their dad, Grandfather Joe, or his brothers. I saw the difference, but I did not comprehend how that difference defined my future.

CHAPTER 5

Learning from Dad

Dad was not one of the boys named "Most Likely to Succeed" in high school. He was active in sports, but his grades were not so good. He was devilish and always into something, like the time he and his friends put some cows in the school one weekend. They confessed and had to clean all of the school, but he was creative in his mischief.

The townsfolk knew that he loved adventure. One day when he was in his late teens, he left home to go on a tramp steamer, and he sailed the Pacific and then came back through the Panama Canal to Miami. He made a salary on this trip and wisely sewed the money inside his jacket so he could keep it safe. He knew the men would steal his money if he didn't hide it.

On another occasion, he and his brother Joe hitchhiked to Kansas to visit family. After they arrived, they worked the family farm to earn money for their return trip home. A neighbor farmer asked them if they would deliver some mules to another farm on their way back to Jensen. Several miles down the road, they had trouble with the mules, so they tied them to a fence post and left them there.

When he was 20 years old, Dad built Jensen Pure Water Company at their home on Church Street. He made wells and water houses and had a truck that delivered five-gallon jugs of water on a regular route of local stores. The water purified as it passed through giant hills of white sand. It was a big success. The water company permit stayed in effect until I abandoned it years later.

Dad ran the RV Camp and built 30 cabins he called the Auto Hotel. He also built Bill's Place on the water, next to the restaurant and filling station. Bill's Place sold fish and was a beer and wine restaurant. In the beginning, Mom worked at Bill's, but later Dad turned it over to Joe and Allan because Grandfather was against Mom working in a place "like that". Grandfather still wanted to control his sons, even though they were grown men. Later, there was some friction in the family because Mom and Dad had a restaurant called Pittman's five miles away in Stuart. Dad had dozens of signs on the highway, leading to his restaurant. Then

Dad owned a hotel called Flamingo. With Pittman's, the hotel, his fish house and several fishing crews he was very successful. They loaded 200-pound barrels of fish onto railroad boxcars by the dozens daily. The fish house was near the ocean inlet on land Dad leased from the county. Anglers could eat and rest there.

I watched Dad in his enterprising efforts. I learned there were good ways to make money and questionable ways to make money. Dad saw Prohibition as an opportunity to provide a desired product to customers. He set up a bootlegging operation, and he was famous for it. Dad's notoriety is remembered on Pitchford Landing "historical photos".

"Capt. Bill Pitchford lived a colorful and legendary life and is remembered for his unique, magnetic personality. His life and adventures were documented in newspaper articles on numerous occasions. Those who knew him believed 'that if all the articles written about him were combined, it would have been a best seller'. He lived life on his terms."

My grandfather did not approve of going against the law and ostracized Dad for conducting business in this way. One afternoon I heard him say, "Bill, you just can't bring that illegal contraband into this country. It is a tarnish on the Pitchford name besides being against the law. I won't have it!"

However, Dad did not see anything wrong with it. "People are going to drink. We can't stop it. Someone will find a way to bring them this stuff, so it might as well be me." Therefore, he continued his business and it was very successful.

My dad did not do things in a small way. He was not a pilot, but he bought airplanes to transport the liquor from the

Bahamas. The planes landed on one of the small airfields in the trees to the west of Jensen. He had enlisted the Seminole Indians to be lookouts for each plane that landed. The Indians would hide in the trees and wave white sheets for the pilot to know that it was safe to land. Dad was friends with the Indians, especially Jack Tommy. Our family stayed friends with Jack Tommy and his family for many years.

During Prohibition, Nassau defied the U.S. again as it had done in the Civil War, ignoring the North's blockade and continuing to trade with Southern states. The island did a lively business smuggling liquor into Southern ports. President Roosevelt repealed the amendment during his administration.

I did not realize that Dad felt that he had to be successful in so many business deals because he was supporting all of his brothers, as well as our family. Dad knew his brothers well and wanted to protect them from their greed.

In some ways, Grandfather set a positive example for his sons. He was a popular and successful, legitimate businessman and was a Sunday School Superintendent at the Congregational Church. He insisted that the house maintain a strict schedule. The housekeeper cleaned weekly and served healthy meals to the family daily. The woman who cooked for him set the "big table". After dinner, she would wash the dishes and then place them back on the table upside down. She made sure that there were always jams and jellies on the sideboard in the dining room.

We were Methodist from my mom's side of the family. Mom, Betty and I went to church on Sundays. Mom was active in the women's groups and made sure that Betty and I attended all the activities for children. Because of our age difference,

Betty and I were involved in separate groups. I think it was here that Betty began to learn how groups could make positive things happen and where she learned how to organize events and recognized this as her calling.

Grandma and Grandpa Lyons attended church with us each week. During the summers, the Leaches, a family from Atlanta came to Sewalls Point. We got to know them pretty well during those summers. They were part of the Coca Cola family and loved being away from Atlanta for the summer. They decided to build a place in North Carolina. They asked Grandpa Lyons to help with building the cabinets for the mansion. It was a sight to see. Their summer property borders Lake Toxaway, near Cashiers, North Carolina. It had a large pool with a pool house where there were extra bathing suits for guests. There was an entertainment room, where visitors could get free Cokes out of a Coke machine. Later, when the Leach family went out of town, Grandma and Grandpa stayed in the guesthouse for the summer. They took care of the family dog, Sugar Pie, who ate canned dog food. This was the first time that I ever saw canned dog food! We were like family with the Leaches. We went to the Methodist Church when we were in Stuart; they also went to the Methodist Church in Stuart and gave a lot of money to that church.

We had a tennis court and Mom loved to play, so did the Leach's oldest daughter. She and Mom enjoyed playing tennis together, but while she was there, she ran our water bill way up because she took such long showers. After her divorce from her first husband, Mrs. Leach decided to move to Palm Beach and sold the mansion to the Catholic Sisters.

In the 1940s, King Edward VIII gave up his throne to marry "the woman I love" and settled in Nassau. The new couple, known as the Duke and Duchess of Windsor, began a new era of peaceful glamor there. They attracted many visitors, celebrities and famous figures to the islands. The Duchess attended the grand opening of the Seminole Inn in Indian Town west of Jensen. Grandfather and Grandmother drove there by horse and buggy.

I guess I must have been about seven or eight years old because my sister was just a tiny thing walking around. We were out with the Indians and one of the Indian women stopped Betty and put a string around her. At the time, we thought that was strange, but we did not think any more about it. A few weeks later, when Dad was out of town on business, here came a flatbed truck full of Indians. Jack Tommy came to our door and asked to see Dad. He had his family and many of his friends with him. Mom said Dad was out of town but should be back the next day. Jack Tommy stood there for a few minutes and said that he really wanted to see Dad. Mom was struggling to communicate with him. Dad did a much better job communicating with Jack Tommy.

Mom and Dad took an annual trip up North to the Adirondacks and had the camper in the yard cleaning it for the trip. It appeared that Jack Tommy was not going to leave with his wife and children. He said they had come a long way and were hungry. Mom went back inside the house to finish preparing for their trip. Later that morning, she looked out the window and the Indians were still in the yard. They turned on the faucet; turned off the faucet; turned on the faucet, etc. Then they turned the lights on; turned the lights off; turned the lights on, etc.

Frustrated, Mom went across the street to the grocery store and bought a variety of cold cuts. The Indians had never eaten processed food, but Jack Tommy and his family enjoyed the cold cuts. When Dad returned that evening, Jack Tommy, his wife and children had settled in. Dad was happy to see them, went over to greet Jack Tommy and his family, and said. "Good to see you."

They gave Dad large tins of huckleberries they had brought. Jack Tommy said that his wife wanted to see my little sister, Betty, and my mother, but she spoke little English. Therefore, he wanted Dad to help her translate for Mom.

Mom and Betty came outside and we met in the yard in front of the camper. Mrs. Jack Tommy took out a package and unveiled an Indian maiden's dress assembled from various shaped pieces of leather with tiny designs on each piece.

She had made the gift for Betty, and it fit her perfectly. Now we knew why one of the Indian women had taken a long strip of string and held it up to Betty, put it around her shoulders, her waist and down to below her knees. We thought it was some kind of Indian ritual, but, in reality, it was measurements for this outfit.

Betty jumped up and down and ran inside to put on the dress.

Jack Tommy said, "We spend night."

Therefore, Mom, gathered sheets, towels and pillows and put them in the camper to give them a comfortable place to sleep for the night. The Indians slept on the floor.

That was a special time for the Jack Tommy family and us. The Seminole Indians' lives wove in and out of ours for many years. One day about 60 years later, I was in the hospital waiting room in Stuart, Florida because my Dad's next oldest brother was having an operation. I kept looking at the only other person in the waiting room. She was beautiful with long black hair. I had to ask her, "Are you Seminole?"

She said, "Yes, I am." We started a conversation and I learned that she was only one week younger than I. She was the last of the Seminole babies born in the woods. Her name was Happy. I will never forget her.

Life was unpredictable and exciting as I grew up. Each day was different from the rest. I never got bored. I was up early each morning to see what adventure I would have that day.

Dad bought his first airplane from a man called Wrong Way Corrigen. Wrong Way got his name because he flew his plane the wrong way in an airplane contest. I remember going to Lake Kissimmee camping where the adult men retrieved the engine out of that crashed airplane.

After WWII, Dad purchased two BT13 planes from the government. He gutted them to haul lobsters from the islands. During those years, the whole town would get together and take the school buses out to shoot wild turkeys. Everyone camped out with the Indian families. They all slept in the buses and the children slept in tents. There were also several beach parties with almost all the town folks attending. The adults built a huge fire on the beach and filled washtubs with Cokes and other soft drinks. They cooked the turkeys over the fire. The men "turtle-watched," and one time they caught a huge loggerhead turtle. The butcher cut it up and divided it among the attendees.

During my youth, there was no such thing as television. We had to entertain ourselves the best way we could. My joy was in nature: the river and the ocean. Eventually, radio was available, and we would all gather around it and listen to programs like "The Inner Sanctum".

Having a sibling did not guarantee that we would be close, even if she is a girl. My little sister, Betty, and I could not have been more different. While I trailed after Dad and wanted to be his shadow, Betty was happier in the house with Mom. She liked school and had good grades. At Palm Beach High she was very popular, participated in a sorority and was the Drum Majorette. Mom was an accomplished seamstress and kept her in the latest fashions.

In the early days, I tolerated her, but she never was happy outside and since I was five years older, she couldn't do all the things my friends and I did each day. We drifted apart as we got older. She and Dad never had a close relationship. He refused to send her to college, although she was an above-average student. His refusal shattered their relationship for many years.

Moving from school to school began early on. When I was going into the first grade, the school in Jensen burned. We had to attend classes in a large commercial building, and then they built the new school, which was a couple of miles south of our house. I attended that school until fourth grade.

Dad had a motorcycle in those days. He would let me sit in front of him on the gas tank and take me to school on the motorcycle. We never did things the traditional way. I can remember helping Dad plant a whole row of pine trees along the side of the new school. We went out into the area of Australian pines where he dug up the saplings, no more than a foot high, and planted them. These were trees that would grow fast and high and would help landscape the new school grounds. He was always doing things for so many town folks. He kept my first and second grade teachers in fresh fish and gave them honey from the beehives.

At our house, the fence posts where the cows grazed were made out of gumbo-limbo limbs and they grew up into great trees. They are still there at over 80 years old.

Dad was not afraid to try anything new. One time when Mom was out of town at a bridge tournament, Dad decided that he would make grape jelly. He had two or three of my friends agree to help him pick the wild grapes, which were across the railroad tracks.

Dad set up his jelly-making place in the garage. He put together a makeshift stove and got the largest pan he could find for the jelly. He cooked the grapes but ended up with only one half-pint milk jar of jelly. We had lots of grape syrup and the garage was a mess and stayed sticky for a long time. Dad had fun trying his hand at something new.

I attended fifth grade in Salerno, about 10 miles south of Jensen. Dad was big in the fishing industry there, so we moved nearby. We had an apartment there for about a year.

In sixth grade, I attended the Northwood School in West Palm Beach. Grandma Lyons had a four-bedroom, stucco, Spanish-style house on the river. Mom, Betty and I stayed with her, because Grandma's house was close to Dad's fishing business, allowing Dad to visit more often. His business was growing and he needed to be near it, but Mom did not like the fishing camp, so eventually we rented an apartment two streets away from Grandma. Dad visited on the weekends. His business was picking up and he was making a lot of money at that time.

It was not easy to change schools so often. There was no continuity in my classes or friends during those years. That may have been one reason that I did not like going to school.

CHAPTER 6

Adventures of a Teen

We moved to Stuart where I attended school from the seventh grade through the 11th grade. Dad became more prosperous there. Mom and Dad owned a very popular restaurant called Pittman's. We also owned the Flamingo Hotel and lived in an apartment on the hotel grounds. I worked at Pittman's as a waitress when I was 13. Stuart was a town of about 5,000 people, six miles from Jensen Beach. Dad owned several businesses, which included the fish house. He bought fish from the fishermen, which he loaded into 200- pound barrels. He shipped the barrels in railroad cars headed to New York. That amounted to thousands of pounds of fish weekly.

Grandpa Lyons tended the front desk at the hotel. When Grandma Lyons passed away, Grandpa Lyons continued to work at the front desk.

There was a period in Stuart, Florida, that was just fun and full of adventure. Chee Chee Ricou, Loraine McPherson, Dee Law, Mary Strange and I explored every inch of our property either on foot or on horses. We all had horses and became proficient with riding. We spent many nights camping in the woods with our horses nearby. We named ourselves the "Buzzards". Chee Chee had two horse, so we used one as a packhorse to carry our supplies. We carried .22 caliber rifles for protection against any wild animals we might encounter. We camped in tents along canal banks, where we caught fish to fry over a fire. We gathered wood our first day so we could keep a fire burning all night. We slept in the sleeping bags on the ground. Often we would hear the panthers howl. Everyone in town knew when we were going on one of our camping trips. We always went to the drugstore, tied our horses out front and ordered sodas on our way out of town. When we returned, my mother would declare that my jeans would stand alone from the dirt.

Eventually, Dad loaned us an old auto with the backend cut out for our camping trips. We drove through the dense woods where there were no roads. Many times, we would have to jack up the "Buzzard Wagon", as we called it, to patch an inner tube.

That was only one side of my personality. Folks in town would say, "That Beverly could be in dirty horse attire, go home, and come out dressed for a prom." I loved being in the woods, but I also loved dressing up in beautiful clothes. Working allowed me to have the money I needed to buy the outfits I wanted and to develop confidence talking to people.

At 13, I waited tables in Mom's restaurant. In 1940, most of the people who came into the restaurant were guests at the hotel. Courtesy and respect directed how I treated the diners. It was important for me to make them happy with their meals and the service. Later, townsfolks would come in to eat because there was not another family restaurant in town. I met many customers during that year and learned how to deal with a variety of temperaments.

At 14, in 1941. I worked as a soda jerk in Davis' Drug Store. It was a fun job. Kids would drop in after school or hang out any time of the day or night during the summer. I heard stories about first dates, sob stories about romantic break-ups, and what teams the boys wanted to play on for baseball or rivalries between football teams. I picked up tips on how to maneuver through many issues.

I was a Girl Scout. We had meetings in the log cabin on the school grounds. It was uneventful. I also played the clarinet in the high school band. We took trips to the Orange Bowl and to the Gasparilla in Tampa each year.

Dad donated all the fish each Friday to the school cafeteria. He also bought the uniforms for the football players. When the number one player's family moved from Stuart, we provided a room at our hotel so he could playout the rest of the year.

Dad bought my aging horse, Blue, for $50.00 and a truck full of cornflakes. The cornflakes came from a salvaged ship torpedoed by the German subs. I also had a pet foot-long alligator. Dad brought it home and I put it in the bathtub until Mother evicted it, so I took it to a football game with its snout tied. That action got me a lot of attention.

In 1942 at age 15, I sold tickets at the Lyric Theater across the Arcade from the drugstore.

It was while working at the Lyric Theater that I had my first boyfriend. He was in the Coast Guard stationed on Jensen Beach. His horse patrol unit watched for German submarines, because subs had torpedoed several large vessels along the coast. I was working at the ticket counter and he would walk past the ticket window and smile at me. Then he wrote notes and sent them to me. This went on for several days. When he started sending me notes about going out with him, I thought he was charming and couldn't resist his request for a date.

We dated for several months, going to the movies, the beach and riding horses bareback in the surf. He was an excellent equestrian from Eastland, Texas, since he was in the horse patrol, and I loved trying to keep up with him on the sand at the beach. I felt free, interesting and pretty. I was heartbroken when he shipped out. I can still see him waving from the troop train. First love usually ends in heartache.

During that time, the Service Club built a building for the military personnel. It gave the men and women a place to come, relax and enjoy the snack bars and dancing. I spent my high school years jitterbugging with those young men. During

WWII, the military allowed us to go to a private club in a military truck, where we sang songs in route to the swimming pool.

Mom and the Stuart Ladies worked the snack bars and chaperoned us. Those years were wonderful, and I was so proud of my mom. She was active in the professional business clubs and owned Pittman's restaurant. She worked hard at the restaurant, but took time to perform civic duties. She taught us it was important to give back to the community part of our money and time. What a beautiful and smart woman she was!

It was about this time that I noticed how Mom and Betty seemed to spend a lot of time together. Mom had Betty in the room, whether sewing clothes or cooking dinner for us. I could hear them talking softly and laughing occasionally. Mom and I had not ever spent time together like that. I noticed it, but it did not bother me.

My life was a fairytale. Like all teenagers, I thought that since my life was magical, the entire family was happy. Honestly, I was so wrapped-up in my life, that I did not really know what was going on with my sister or Mom and Dad.

The summer after my 11th grade, our family fell apart! My sister, Betty attended music camp in Brevard, North Carolina. Mother and I went with her and Mom stayed in a lovely lodge in Brevard. I attended Brevard Jr. College to finish my high school requirements. I needed an English course and one other elective course in order to graduate. I completed those courses and graduated with a high school diploma from Brevard Jr. College in September 1943, at age16.

CHAPTER 7

It's Not All It Seems

Dad came to Brevard a couple of times to visit. When the day came for the three of us to return to Stuart, Dad came up and drove Mom home. Betty and I rode the train later. Betty and I were surprised because we all three had tickets to return home by train.

Dad said, "Wanda, I thought I'd surprise you and you and I could drive home together and let the girls go on the train as you planned."

Mom smiled and being used to Dad's spontaneity said, "That would be lovely. There is a little restaurant on the way home, where we could stop for a late lunch, or early dinner."

This was not a celebratory trip. On the way home, Dad confessed to Mom that he had been seeing someone else while Mom was gone. He declared that it was over.

It was not. Mom and Dad separated and later that year Mom and Betty moved to West Palm Beach. It was a sad time for us. My friends were starting their senior year of high school, but at age 16, I had already graduated from Brevard Jr. College, so I went to work in the Western Union office. The only other person in the office was Millie, the wife of a military man. She and I became friends in a short while. I confided in her about my family situation.

She tried to cheer me up, "Sometimes things work out in a way that upsets us. Just continue to love your parents and find your own way in the world. You are young and have so much life to live. I'm sure things will work out for the best if you keep a positive outlook."

Unexpectedly, her husband received orders to move to another location. Western Union asked me to run the local office, but when I worked alone in that office I became very depressed. I tried to heed what Millie had said, but I was young and inexperienced. I was not happy with the job and its responsibilities and I was dealing with my parents' separation. I only worked there from September 1944 until January 1945.

I was so disappointed in Dad and mad at him. I could not believe that he would act out this way; I thought he and Mom had a good marriage. I was naïve, as most children are about their parent's lives. I learned later, that Mom was not always happy with Dad's decisions. She was upset that he included his brothers in all of his business undertakings. It was like they were riding on his shoulders. One time, I did hear an argument between them about a new business Dad started. Mom was begging him to let the business just be his and hers and not a Pitchford family business. He was insistent that he had to carry the Pitchford dynasty forward as the oldest of the six sons.

"It's my responsibility to share my success with my brothers. I am the oldest. They look to me for guidance. We have plenty. Why are you so against sharing it with the family?"

She responded, "I want something to be ours. You work hard and have creative ideas. They have formal educations. They should be able to support themselves and take care of their own needs."

Even as a young girl, I thought it was odd that my Dad felt he had to take care of his brothers. They were more educated than he was and had more opportunity to make a good living. Grandfather Pitchford never forgave Dad for selling bootleg whiskey, would not trust him with making decisions for the Pitchford family and eventually turned to Doc for that help. I did not know that this was a preview of what life would be like for the Pitchford men. They were beginning to give up and look to someone else to provide for them.

As I learned later, the separation and later divorce of Mom and Dad was the beginning of Dad's loss of oversight of the Pitchford's dynasty. His diversion with his mistress caused him to miss signs that Doc (one of Dad's brothers) was influencing Grandfather to give him control of the property. It was Doc and his wife's goal to own all of the Pitchford property. The first step was to control Grandfather, which he was doing now that Dad was out of the picture. Grandfather had already begun selling off property to pay the bills. When Doc got control of the checkbook, he irresponsibly sold property on a whim. Grandfather eventually moved to West Palm Beach and Doc took complete control of the finances, ignoring taxes and maintenance of the property. Grandfather died in 1959.

I thought that Dad was a little insecure about not having a college education. I assumed he might have felt that he made a bad decision when he chose to skip further formal learning. Some of that doubt translated to how he felt about my future after the rupture of our family.

Dad did not want me to stop my education and wanted me to get to know Mom's family, so he sent me to Springfield Catholic Jr. College in Illinois the following January, 1944. At that point, I did not really care about what I did. I was so disillusioned.

I lived with the nuns during the week and on the weekends lived with Aunt Nonie or Cousin Dorothy. I tried to think of it as an adventure. On leaving Stuart, I had to take a train to Chicago and change trains to get down to Springfield. The train ride from the flatland country of Jensen, Florida, was my first trip out of the South. I kept my eyes peeled to the window most of the way. I fell in love with the lush countryside. The wild azaleas and dogwoods grew willy-nilly deep in the woods. Miles of pasture with cows, or horses or goats popped between the woodlands. When we drew close to large cities, I wanted to pull the rope on the train and disembark into this new world of activity. I connected with the tall buildings and busy roads. I loved the energy of the pedestrians on sidewalks, darting here and there. I wondered where these people were going. Why were they in a hurry? It was so different from my laid-back life in Florida.

When we finally reached Chicago, there was no holding me back. My curious and adventurous nature got the better of me. The urge to see the city was too strong. Therefore, I stored my suitcase in the safe at the station and took a taxi to the Loop. I was not accustomed to the cold and had never worn stockings. I was freezing. I immediately stopped at a store and bought my first pair of stockings and a garter belt.

Surprisingly, I loved everything at school, even the cold weather. I met two girls, Sybil and Gloria, who became my best friends. Dad felt guilty about the family break-up, so he sent 200 pounds of fish to the nuns, which added to my popularity. It was so cold that Cousin Dorothy helped me pick out my first fur coat. When we left the store, we heard that President Roosevelt had died. Life was full of changes and adjustments.

Sybil's family had a spacious lake house where we had fun parties some weekends. Gloria and I shared a love of horses and frequently rode in the lush park on horses we rented. Getting back to something familiar and being in nature on our horses distracted me. This activity made it easier for me to endure the week of studies.

The three of us had a favorite café in town where we went on Saturdays. It was a quaint brownstone with three small rooms and a large kitchen. Most of the restaurant was dark, where couples would meet discreetly, but we sat in the front room with full windows and looked out at the Saturday hustle and bustle of a big city. On each visit, we ordered sliced chicken sandwiches and Singapore Slings. We thought we were big dogs. My new friends and these adventures helped heal the hurt from what my dad had done.

I had never had close female friendships where you talk about boys and personal things, but I felt so close to Gloria and Sybil that I shared my parent's separation with them.

"I thought that when you married, it was for life. I can't believe that Dad can just go off with another woman."

Sybil smiled coyly, "Men have physical needs and when your Mom was gone for those months he looked for someone to fill that need. It is not love you know. It's lust."

Hearing those words made me want to cover my ears. I could not think about my Dad being with another woman in that way.

Sybil continued, "Several of my parent's friends are divorced or cheating on each other. It is not unheard of. It's the way of our changing times."

I could see that happening in her societal world, but not my world in Jensen Beach. Her comments did help me in an unsettling way.

Mom and Betty came up for a couple of weeks when I was in Springfield. We went to Columbus with Aunt Nonie to visit Aunt Laddie and family. It was about 500 miles away, but we enjoyed our visit in their lovely home. The trip with Mom and Betty was the first time the three of us had been together for a long stretch of time. I noticed that Mom and Betty would huddle, heads close together, and whisper-talk.

Occasionally I could hear a comment or two. "We need to get started on your gown for the Rainbow celebration. What color do you want to wear this time?" Mom asked.

"Let's go with pink; my blonde hair looks good with pink." Betty replied.

Other conversations seemed more personal, more about things that happen as girls reach puberty. I do not remember having those conversations with Mom.

I was happy that Mom wasn't grieving over Dad or mad about how her life had changed. I watched her looking out the window and got the impression that Mom was happy to see the greenery of her home state. The trip to Columbus offered views of fields, hills and green grass everywhere. Somewhere, deep inside her, I saw Mom relax and I hoped that she breathed in the vision of a new life.

While they were visiting, I saw a faraway look in Mom's eyes from time to time. I wondered if she missed Dad. They had seemed so happy. My idea about trust changed completely. I knew what Dad had done was wrong morally, but selfishly I wished Mom had not separated from him. I did not like it that Dad had been pushed to the background in my life. After the weekend with Aunt Nonie, Mom and Betty headed back to Stuart.

I was still mad at Dad because of the divorce. He tried to make amends by sending me $50 a week for my expenses, and taking care of my overdrawn checks each month. I loved my dad and appreciated his financial help, but when I found out that he had bought his mistress a brand new red convertible, I felt betrayed. I asked a friend who lived in Stuart, Florida to secretly take the spark plugs out of that car so that it would not start! I do not know if Dad ever figured out who caused that mischief. He probably did.

Dad's affair turned into a time bomb for him. Mom and Dad's divorce was not final for two years. During those years, Dad wrote Mom several letters saying he was sorry. He even sent her a newspaper article about how common it was for men to "cheat" because of their physical needs and how their wives were not accommodating them. Letters or articles didn't soften Mom toward what he had done; he was still with his mistress. He later married the wench. In the next few years, she spent him into financial ruin and almost broke him. When he caught her cheating on him, they had a terrible quarrel. Dad disappeared to Mexico on the ruse of conducting some business and did not return until she left town with her lover. Dad divorced her.

Dad was his old adventurous self for the next years. He purchased a 60-foot sea-going schooner that slept 12, named the Ranger, and hired two Bahamian crewmembers. He treasure hunted, sometimes with the Bahamian government; his moniker was' Trader Bill'.

I think Dad always had a roving eye for another, more challenging, liaison. Dad met an English woman, Marjorie, who had inherited a failing inn/café. Her husband owned a chain of drug stores in England, but he was a drunkard. She was intrigued with Dad and their friendship grew into a special connection. She divorced her husband, and she and Dad married and sailed away for the summer on Ranger with her two children. At the start of the school year, she sent the children back to England to continue their education.

Even though she had been part of the social life in England, she was intrigued with Dad's primitive way of life

60

and loved living on the schooner. Dad had finally met his soul mate. During a hurricane, they moored in a cove on Captiva Island for safety. Apparently, they loved it so much that they built a house on the island. After a few years, I guess wanderlust waned, because they sold that house and moved back to Jensen into the house that Mom and Dad had built. They were married until Dad died.

I did not want his new wife in my life, so I distanced myself from Dad even more. It was at this time that I realized something about my Dad. While he had grandiose ideas, he frequently did not follow-through with a project. Sometimes he sold his ideas, but usually he abandoned them when they became difficult and left them for something new. This was the first time I had the realization that Dad gave up when the going got tough.

After completing courses at the Catholic Jr. College in Springfield, I headed back to Florida to attend Palm Beach Jr. College. The train had a stopover in St. Louis, Missouri, and when the train started up again the news came that the War was over! That train became a huge party with singing, dancing in the aisles and some drinking. A handsome Air Force Lieutenant sat across the aisle from me and soon we became friends. It was a case of good, clean admiration. He wrote to me from Salt Lake City several times and I responded before I got busy with college. He was a hard one to forget.

There were a few other young men in my life briefly during my 17th and 18th years. One in particular, Jerry Thomas, took me to lovely dinners. Another young man, Stratton Jamison, was a year ahead of me in high school. He was in the Marines and went to Iwo Jima. When he returned after the war, he wanted to marry me and even asked my Dad's permission, but I wasn't in love with him.

I stopped in Stuart, Florida, and stayed with Mom and Betty until September, when I went to Palm Beach Jr. College. It felt strange to be back in Stuart where Dad was, but I never initiated a visit with him. Mom, Betty and I kept to ourselves and did not interact with the rest of the Pitchford family. Much of the time, I felt like a visitor with them, because they had long conversations, went shopping and cooked together. I was not part of those times.

While in Stuart, I attended the "victory dance" at Camp Murphy, celebrating the end of the war. As I started up the steps of the USO, someone yelled, 'Boots'. When I turned, I saw a boy I had met at the bowling alley in Springfield. Randy remembered that I had told him to call me Boots. He became a regular date for most of the year. I lived at the YWCA for a while until Mom and Betty moved to our new house in West Palm Beach.

I did learn that Dad had cut the brothers off from any of his new businesses. He certainly had bad timing.

I was a "good" girl in the midst of my impulsiveness. I wasn't a drinker, except for the Southern Comfort that Chee Chee brought when we were young and camped out in the winter cold in Stuart and the Singapore Slings I drank on Saturdays with Sybil and Gloria in Illinois. In addition, I only stole one thing in my life. When the Buzzards dared me, I snuck a corn cobb pipe from the dime store in Stuart.

CHAPTER 8

Life of a Young Pan American Woman

1945 (age 18)

Early in my 18th year, I worked for Major Birdsail, in a real estate office on County Road in Palm Beach.   When his son got out of the service, he decided to build houses. His first house was on Mira Flores Drive in Palm Beach. I almost felt a part of his project because he had house plans spread all over my desk. One day he was getting frustrated because he could not find a new refrigerator for one of the houses he was ready to sell.

I spoke up and said, "I'll call my dad. He knows everyone in this area. Maybe he can help find a refrigerator for you."

Dad was excited to hear from me. "Hey Bev, how are you?" When I told him about the situation with the refrigerator, he said, "Sure. I'll be happy to look for a refrigerator to help your boss." He came through for me and found one in a store in Stuart.

Young Birdsail was thankful that I helped him and went to Stuart to pick it up. Today, Birdsail is a very large construction company. It grew out of the determination and creativity of the Birdsail family. This was the first time that I reached out to Dad and he was there for me. I only worked for this company for a short while, but I believed that this job led me back to my Dad.

I heard that a couple of girls from Stuart were working at Morrison Field Air Force Base. I wanted to work there too. Luckily, there was an opening in the Personnel Office. My job was to be in charge of the timecards for all the workers on the aircraft lines. There were workers all the way across to the other side of the field. I had a Jeep and a driver named Dizzy. He was something—not a tooth in his head—and he was always laughing. He drove me all over the airfield. He kept me laughing because of his good nature and ability to find humor in everything he did.

One day I met my Dad at the airport, which seemed to be our normal place to visit. It was after he married his mistress, so the airport was a "free-zone" for our meetings. He had flown in on a Delta flight from Tallahassee. He spent a good bit of time on the trip talking with one of the flight attendants. She told him about her exciting life as a stewardess and that intrigued my adventure-seeking father. I could still see the excitement on his face. He said, "That would be an interesting job for you. But you're not old enough."

Immediately, I bought into that idea and said, "That's exactly what I'm going to do." Boredom had set in and I needed to move on. I wanted some excitement in my life.

Dad said, "You can't do that! You cannot work for Delta. You're only 18." Well, because I wanted to prove to Dad that I could be just as daring as he, I went to the airport the next morning, got on an airplane for the first time in my life and flew to Miami to apply for a job.

When I got to the Delta personnel office, I filled out the application and went in for an interview. At the end of the interview, the recruiter said, "I would love to hire you. I love your energy and upbeat personality, but you are too young. I cannot hire an 18 year-old. Come back in a couple of years."

I left disappointed, but decided there was no harm in seeking an interview with Pan American. Luckily, they also were interviewing that day. Their application was a little lengthier. The interviewer started out with the same kind of statements. "I'd love to hire you, but you're too young."

I let tears roll down my face and I said, "I took Spanish in high school and at Springfield Catholic Junior College." I overheard they needed Spanish speaking flight attendants to fill their Latin American Run.

He smiled at me and asked, "When is your birthday?"

My response was, "Soon. In a couple of months."

He shook his head and held out his hand to shake mine. "Okay, you're hired." I held the record for the youngest stewardess at Pan Am.

I could pretty much maneuver things to my liking. For some reason, it came natural for me to know what to say and how to act with people to accomplish what I set out to do, with the help of that angel on my shoulder.

The first day I dressed in a Pan American uniform, I stood before the mirror in awe of my professional appearance. The blue knee length skirt and buttoned suit jacket was set off by the white cotton collared blouse. The military cap completed the entire look and gave me confidence that I could do a good job. I was honored and proud to wear the uniform. Everything about this day felt right.

My home base was Miami. In the beginning my flights were to Nassau, back to Miami and then to Havana, Cuba, all within the same day! Then I graduated to the North Coast Run, which ran from Trinidad to Panama and back with stops along the way. Up until now, my experiences tested me about my comfort with uncertainty. These decisions taught me how to develop and grow a business even though I was just having fun. I was a young girl, not worldly in any sense and I entered the magic world of travel and adventure.

I believe that God puts certain people in our lives just when we need them. Some remain in our life for a long time, even though we may not see them often.

Others are there for a season and then as you grow, move on.

That is the way my relationship with my stewardess sorority was. I had not had a traditional matriculation through my school years and my relationship with my mom was not close. In time, these young women became my mentors, friends and confidants.

CHAPTER 9

Jack's Early Years

1923 – 1946 (Jack)

Jack and I enjoyed each other's company. Sometimes we sat on my mother's porch and talked about our lives as children and teenagers. I wanted Jack to know everything about my life, so, I shared many stories about my parents, grandparents and extended family.

I knew Jack would enjoy stories about my dad, who was as unpredictable as Jack was. There was always one adventure or another. I got my zest for life from my dad.

One lazy Sunday afternoon as we sat on Mom's patio, I pulled out photo albums. "Jack, would you like to see pictures of Dad and the Pitchford family?"

Mom brought out a pitcher of lemonade and two glasses, "I thought you might enjoy a cold drink while you visit." She discretely went back inside. She didn't want to distract us. I wanted Jack to hear my interpretation of our lives when Betty and I were growing up.

"Jack, over the years you will hear many accounts of my life, but I want you to hear about it from my perspective," I said as I lifted the cover and looked at the first photos. Memories flooded back to those wonderful days. There was never a dull moment around my dad. My part in that began the day I was born.

I embellished my birth story with lavish descriptions of the drive to the hospital. Dad tried to hide from Mom how scared he was. Mom had told me all the details many times over my life. I also shared with Jack the story about my grandmother who was in the hospital at the same time as my birth, "Several weeks before I was born, the family was going to a ball game. On the way down the stairs, Grandmother Pitchford suddenly lost feeling in her foot and fell to the floor. The hospital staff diagnosed her with a fatal illness called 'creeping paralysis'. She was bedridden for several months and was still in the hospital the night I was born."

I continued with a description of Dad's family. "My grand-parents had six boys. The story goes that, when Grandmother found out I was a girl she could not wait to hold me. Mother took me down to her room in the hospital and gently handed me to her. Mom said that the twinkle in Grandmother's eyes showed how thrilled she was to have a girl in the family. Sadly, Grandmother only lived three months after I was born."

Jack and I were getting very comfortable with each other. We hated the end of the weekends when we had to part. Those were wonderful summer days when we both landed in West Palm Beach and spent our time at Mom's house. The days were both relaxing and intriguing. It was a small, white blockhouse, but the front yard was completely level with a swooping palm tree at the right corner, and a short paved driveway on the left, and was an oasis in the heat of summer. We hung out on the back patio in comfortable loungers under the awnings. During these times, I learned about Jack's life.

He began by telling me that he was born on May 5, 1923, on Venable Street in Atlanta, Georgia, at home. Dr. Cousins delivered him and perfunctorily placed him in a dresser drawer. His parents divorced when he was seven. His mother worked at The Atlanta Journal and they lived with his grandparents. He saw his father a few times when he was 18.

His grandfather worked for the railroad and got up at 5 a.m. His grandmother got up earlier than that to cook him whole-wheat biscuits, because he had heart trouble and could not digest white flour. His grandmother tended to a large garden in the side yard; they had plenty of fresh vegetables to eat.

Jack went to Luckie Street Elementary School, which was about four blocks from Georgia Tech College and four blocks from his grandparents' home. They attended the Methodist church, which was only two blocks away. The Vice President of Luckie Street School knew someone at Coca Cola and often wrote notes to him. She asked Jack to take the notes to her friend, knowing that it would be safe for a six-foot boy to walk the six blocks alone. Jack did not mind this task at all, because each time he went to the Coca Cola office, he received a free fountain Coke to drink.

He and his friends would walk on the cobblestone sidewalks to Georgia Tech, watch the sports teams practice and sometimes even work as batboys. During that time, everyone had roller skates and skated wherever they could. Jack roller-skated on the basketball court at Georgia Tech because the floors were so smooth. After their games, he would pick up Coke bottles and turn them in for cash. After elementary school, he went to O'Keefe High School and then transferred to Boys High for two years. Finally, he attended Tech High and took courses in flight mechanics because he loved airplanes.

The home on Venable Street was in a prestigious neighborhood. His grandmother was very happy there, but his grandfather died when Jack was fourteen and he and his grandmother could not afford to stay in the home, so they moved into a small house on Virginia Highland Avenue. His grandmother was not happy with this house, but Jack liked its coziness.

He was head usher at the Lowe's Grand Theater at night. The streetcar cost $.05 each way and he earned $14/week. During the summer when he was 18, he worked at Globe Finance at night in the collections department and tried to get folks to bring their account current, paying from one dollar to three dollars weekly on their accounts. His mother had remarried and his stepdad was the Advertising Manager of the Atlanta Journal.

At Tech High, Dr. Chancy let Jack graduate four days early because he joined the U.S. Army Air Corps and had to leave before the scheduled last day of class. He went to Keesler Air Force Base, where one of his first jobs as a recruit was to wash garbage cans. He told his sergeant, "I don't like this assignment. I'm qualified to do much more than this!"

His sergeant replied, "You're in the military now, and your **job** is whatever you are told to do, without complaint!"

Jack needed patience because there was a waiting period before he could go to pilot training. The Army finally sent him to Century College in Shreveport, where he received 10 hours of training in a Piper Cub.

There was a party at the Base serving ice cream to military personnel. Jack was impatient to get into the party, but there was a long line at the door. Jack told the sergeant on duty at the door that he and his two friends, Jack Marr and Fagan Raider, were professional soda jerks and could help move the line along. Therefore, they entered the room and were placed at the serving table. In theory, they would take orders for sodas, banana splits and sundaes as well as plain scoops of ice cream.

They became overwhelmed with the number of people in line demanding service. They agreed that they would only serve one item: vanilla ice cream with chocolate syrup on it in a dish. They set up a serving line where each one of them would only handle one job. The first person added one scoop of vanilla ice cream into a cup; handed it to the next person, who would add the chocolate syrup; and the last person took the money. Folks were complaining and yelling that they were getting the wrong order, but the three boys just kept producing the ice cream in that way until the line was gone. At the end, they decided they didn't want to ever serve ice cream again!

Jack was a fun-loving guy, but his training taught him to follow the rules. Not everyone he met felt the same way. Good Fellow Field in St. Angelo, Texas was the location for basic training. The small airfield had board sidewalks. His first plane was a PT 19, Fairchild Open Cockpit. The instructor was a Texan who drove a big yellow Cadillac and wore a ten-gallon hat. He donated his time to train the pilots, because he was an expert pilot and the military trainers were on active duty in the war.

In advanced training, Jack moved from base to base to get experience on every plane available to the Air Force. They included a closed cockpit BT 13 with a radio engine and increased horsepower. Then came the AT6, which had radio engines, a cockpit that slid over the pilot and retractable wheels. Jack's instructor had some fun with him while training on the P40 in Illinois. He had one afternoon of training how to fly the gliders. Early the next morning he went back for additional training. Jack and another trainee sat waiting on the instructor to come in for glider pilot training.

The trainer came into the room and demanded, "Why are you two men sitting here?" Jack said, "We're waiting on the instructor for glider training."

The sergeant said, "Didn't you learn how fly the glider yesterday?"

Jack responded, "Yes."

Then the sergeant said, "Well, then you're going to train this young airman today."

Jack said he was dumbfounded, but took the plane out and showed the other pilot how to pull and fly the glider.

From there Jack received orders to a ferry command based in Memphis, Tennessee.

Jack received additional advanced training in Eagle Pass, Texas where he received a brand new plane to deliver to the Brazilian Government. He had a stopover in Puerto Rico, before heading to Natal, Brazil. While making his final approach to land in Puerto Rico, he noticed a beat-up plane on the same flight pattern on his left wing. After landing, he ran into that pilot admiring Jack's new plane. As they talked, Jack found out that the other pilot had a flight plan to China. The other pilot expressed concern that the plane would not make it to China using the outdated navigational instruments in his plane.

Jack asked, "Why are you going to China?"

The other pilot said, "I'm a retired military pilot who can't find a job. I have to support my family somehow. So I collect clothes to sell in China to make money to live on."

Jack looked inside and saw that the plane packed with clothes.

In the morning when Jack went to the airfield to fly his plane the remainder of the trip to Natal, he discovered that the other pilot had swapped navigational equipment. He had taken the brand new equipment and put it on his old plane for his trip to China. Jack was happy to help the retired service man make it to China with new equipment.

When Jack delivered the new plane with old navigational equipment to the Brazilian Government, they were delighted and never knew that it had outdated navigational equipment on the new plane.

Jack's new training was on the PQ14, an experimental plane that flew by radio controls, located on huge racks behind the pilot. The equipment was so large that the plane could only hold the pilot, so training was "by the seat of your pants". On his training flight from Dallas to Nashville, the gas tanks were running low, so Jack landed at an airfield to swap out the tanks. There were no other full tanks of gasoline available to swap out at this airfield. The remainder of the trip was sketchy and Jack ended up with an empty tank and crashed his plane into a power line. When he got out of the plane, an old farmer who was driving by in a beat-up flatbed car picked him up, and took him to a hospital. The crash messed his knees and legs up, sprained his ankle and cut his head. He was in the hospital in California for a month. His head injury left a grey streak in his hair forever.

In those days, the military frequently recruited experienced civilian pilots, who trained by unconventional methods. There were pilots who flew their own private planes for crop-dusting or other small non-military jobs, and joined the Army Air Corps to fly for the United States. They were the barnstorming, bush pilots. One of those pilots scheduled a trip to California with Jack. The night before the flight, Jack prepared the flight plan and studied the maps from Nashville to California. When the two pilots met the next morning, Jack pulled out his maps and flight plan to review with the bush pilot who said, "I don't need all that stuff."

Jack replied, "What do you mean you don't need this information. It's a long flight to California."

The bush pilot pulled on his cap and walked out to the plane. "I've flown this route too many times to count. I don't need maps and flight plans. I know exactly how to fly from here to there. Are you coming?"

There was nothing left for Jack to do but to get on the plane, which did make it to California without a hitch.

Jack's closest lifetime friend was McGovern. Mac was very athletic and had been on the tumbling team for the University of Oklahoma. He could do tumble sets all the way down the street. He and Jack started in the Military together and shared many experiences. One time they were driving from California to New England to go to a new assignment. They decided to stop off at Mac's house in Oklahoma where Mac's family had a dairy farm. He coerced Jack into getting on a horse. Once on the horse, it turned around and galloped back to the barn. Jack could not get it to go where he wanted it to go, but the horse took him for a good ride. Mac came and visited with us a couple of times, once at Eglin and years later on Cleary Road in West Palm Beach. We talked about getting together again. Then a short time later, he passed away with stomach cancer. It happened quickly.

Jack's comfort with taking chances was the trait he found in me that drew him to me. I was never afraid to seek adventure and take chances when it appealed to my sensibilities.

I had flown for Pan Am less than a year when I met Jack. Flying was something that satisfied my need for challenges and adventure at that moment. In reality, it was the decision that helped me grow up and be ready for my next adventure, which was with Jack. Boy did we ever have an adventure-filled life!

It was almost pre-ordained that Jack and I would fall in love and marry in an unconventional way. That is what my parents did.

CHAPTER 10

Marriage Surprise

1947 (age 20)

I was enjoying the variety in my Pan Am job from August 1945 until September 1947. Most of the time on the North Coast Run there were repeat passengers. I learned a lot about them from those long, slow flights. It took 71 hours for the DC3 plane to cross from New York to Buenos Aires. Therefore, we had many layovers.

On one flight, Bob Hope and his family boarded in Puerto Rico. Mrs. Hope asked me where I shopped in Buenos Aires. After landing, she went to the shop I recommended. She was so happy with the handmade shoes in that store that on the flight home she gave me a beautiful white purse. She bought it for me as a gift for telling her about the shop. Mr. Hope had enjoyed the pineapples on the island so much that he bought one for all the passengers on the flight. I was with the Hope family for two days. We stopped overnight at Belem, Brazil, where I left them, because I had to lay over and they headed to Rio.

There was a closeness of passengers on these flights. Sometimes I had several hours to sit and visit with them. I became friends with many of them. As we landed in Caracas, Venezuela, a man who had been a passenger asked us if we had ever seen *all* of Caracas.

He said, "Ladies, I know you fly into here often, but have you ever seen all of Caracas? I have a weekend break from my job in the local oil fields, and I would love to show you the 'real Caracas'. Since there were three of us, flight attendants, we felt safe taking him up on his offer. "We'd love it."

He took us to seedy places that most tourists would not see, but then we walked down some of the most beautiful palm-lined walkways where we could see the beach. Next, we absorbed the glamorous side of the city with hundreds of lights hanging from gutters and roofs of the clubs. Calypso music permeated the night air. Pedestrians danced down the streets, holding various intoxicating drinks in the air. The magic of that night would forever color my impression of Caracas.

About the first of July, Jack came down to Miami with some pretty bad news. His new orders transferred him to Mobile, Alabama. They were closing the base in West Palm Beach.

Jack said, "I don't know how we're going to be able to see each other. It will be difficult with me over in Alabama." We were both upset about this situation.

A couple of days later, I went into the office to check-in before my next trip. On the bulletin board there was a note asking volunteers to transfer to Houston, Texas. Without a second thought, I walked over and put my name down. I really didn't think through this decision, but acted on instinct as I often did. Pan Am accepted my request, so I immediately called Jack and told him that I had asked for a transfer to Houston and Pan Am wanted me to leave on July 15, 1947.

Pan Am had a rule that we could not fly to a new assignment. We traveled by train to transport us to our new home base. Jack and Mother took me to the train. Since Jack had lost his car playing pool (the same way he had won it), Mother took him by to pick up his laundry and then dropped him off at the base.

The train had to travel through Mobile on its route to Houston. When we made the stop in Mobile on July 16, Jack was standing there waving me off the train. I rushed to meet him, but I secretly knew he was going to be there.

He had checked into the Battle House Hotel in Mobile. During dinner, I decided to stay with him that night at the hotel. That was the most romantic dinner and tender, sweet night I had ever spent; it was my first experience of perfect love.

On July 17 after breakfast, we went for a walk around Mobile. We were passing a quaint little jewelry store when Jack took my hand and said, "Let's get married!"

He bought me a wedding band and we spent the day preparing for a ceremony, but there was a two-day waiting period to get a marriage license.

We did a little negotiations and the clerk said, "These kids don't need a two-day waiting period." He gave us the license right then.

We arranged to get married in the chapel at the base with Rev. Hope and his wife. It wasn't a lavish event, but in those days, most people didn't have time or money to plan a large wedding. I never regretted getting married this way. In just a few hours, I had to get on the train to continue my trip to Houston.

When we reached New Orleans, I had a 'wait over', so I called my mother and said, "Mom, Jack and I got married in Mobile."

Later, Betty told me that she was standing beside Mom when I called and watched her almost faint. She slid down the wall to the floor. When she recovered, she put wedding announcements and my picture in every paper in and around West Palm Beach and Stuart.

Mom and I became closer after Jack and I married. Several years later, Mom met a wonderful man, Frank Soper, who owned a jewelry store in West Palm Beach. Mom had worked at a jewelry store since she and Dad divorced and that's how she met Frank. They married and I was glad to see Mom so happy. She and Frank visited us from time to time and we had time to develop the relationship I always wanted with her.

In Houston, I went to the Rice House and checked in as Beverly Pitchford for Pan Am. I didn't feel like going out to dinner by myself on my wedding night, so I called room service and ordered a bowl of soup. Just as I finished my soup, there was a knock at the door. When I opened it, there stood Jack!

"How did you get here?" I said.

"When I told my commanding officer that I had just gotten married, he said, 'Boy take a plane and go over to Houston. You can't leave your wife on your wedding night.'" Jack had taken an air force plane on a "training flight" to Houston. You cannot do that kind of thing these days!

Our one-night honeymoon was perfect because I was with the man I loved. After Jack left the next day, June 20, I checked in with Pan American, as required. Stewardesses could not be married; therefore, I also gave them my two-week notice, because that was the proper way to resign. That also allowed me to get my back pay for the previous two weeks.

My assignment was to fly to Panama from Houston and then across the North Coast of South America. My first flight from Houston was a straightforward flight down to Panama with stops in Mexico City and Guatemala and a couple of other places. The first leg of the flight was okay, but after that, we had problems. Every time I would get on a plane, we had either engine problems or some other major issue, so Pan Am would change my flight. As a result, my two weeks turned out to be longer because the plane had problems three times. Finally, I was in Mexico City. I did not know what to do, but I was hoping I was going back to Houston on the next airplane.

I was out on the flight line when I saw a purser (a male steward), Kerry Anderson, someone I knew. I said, "Kerry, my uniforms are getting dirty because I haven't been home in three weeks. I want to get back to Houston. Would you switch flights with me?"

He said, "Yes, I'll do that" Well, 'lo and behold', his flight wasn't going back to Houston. His destination was Mata Mores, which is on the border of Mexico and the United States. By that time, I was talking to the crew who lived there. It was late when we got in to Mata Mores, so they said, "Why don't you come and spend the night with us? We have a house."

I felt more secure staying with them than trying to find a hotel in Mata Mores. Pan Am always selected our hotels and paid for them. We stayed in the very best rooms, because Pan Am wanted to make a good impression in foreign countries. I did go with the three pilots and spent the night, but I had my own room and I locked the door. The next day they took me over to the airport and I deadheaded to Houston. I went out to where I was living and picked up my things and got a plane to Mobile, Alabama. That was the end of my Pan American career.

When I got to Mobile, it was two months after Jack and I married.

CHAPTER 11

Another Life Change

1948 (age 21)

Before I arrived in Mobile, Jack found a little house for us to rent. He had that all set up before I got there. I had not met any of Jack's family at this time. His mother came to Mobile and we went with her to New Orleans for the weekend. She was going to visit with her new daughter-in-law. We had a nice dinner with her and she and I got along immediately. We took her back to the hotel and Jack and I went night clubbing. It was kind of like a honeymoon for us. We recorded our "late honeymoon" with many pictures at one of the clubs and had a great time.

We enjoyed the months together in our first little house in Mobile. It was September when I got there. In October, we went to Halloween parties and I met several of Jack's friends. Every day Jack brought home one of his friends to our house for lunch. He did not have a car then, but they always loaned him cars. I made oyster stew that Jack thought was wonderful, which meant that we had oyster stew every day for lunch. We always could count on wonderful seafood from Mobile Bay.

Jack said, "Bev your oyster stew is so delicious, I want to share it with my friends. Are you okay with me bringing them here for lunch? That way they drive and I get to see you in the middle of the day." It was a treat for me to see him in the middle of the day, too.

We were only there September and October of 1947. Before the first of November, Jack received a transfer to Goose Bay, Labrador, for one year. No family could go because there were no living quarters for family.

Jack was distraught about his orders, "Bev, I hate to leave you. We're just starting our life together!"

I did not want him to go either. I had grown up with my dad disappearing for long periods of time when he was doing one project or another. Mom seemed to handle the separation graciously. I wanted to do that for Jack. I could not have him leave with me sobbing and hanging on to him. That wasn't my style anyway. I knew I would face separation repeatedly with

Jack, just has I had with Dad, but Jack had no control over those separations. Dad did.

Before Jack left, we went to Atlanta to spend a few days with his mother and stepfather, Bill Cunningham. They were so welcoming to me that I decided to stay in Atlanta while Jack was serving his time in Goose Bay. One night as we shared stories of our lives, Jack's mom shared, "Jack always had a love of airplanes. I don't know where that came from. When he was just a little boy—maybe four or five—he would sit behind a fan on the porch and pretend to be a pilot flying a plane."

With a knowing smile, I said, "I love that story. I can picture him doing that with his face lit up with his enticing smile."

After I was in Atlanta a few weeks, I saw an ad for a secretary at Georgia Tech in the military department. Because of the variety of office jobs I had held, working as a stewardess and marrying a Georgia Tech man who was serving our country, I got the job and worked for Col. Jeffords at Georgia Tech from January 1948 until January 1949. Col. Jeffords had a distinguished career in the Army and he was well known.

At 21 years old, it was a good place for me to work. One of the big social events that occurred during the time I worked for Col. J (his nickname), at Georgia Tech, Fort McPherson held a banquet and dance. Col. J asked me if I would go with him and his girlfriend. I said, "I'm honored that you asked me."

Mrs. Sampson, who lived next door to Jack's mother, made me a beautiful dress to wear with a headband to match. It was the first time I had gone to a dance since Jack left and I had a good time because I loved to dance and several men asked me to dance. One of the men asked me to go with him to a party at another house.

I said, "You'll have to ask Col. J."

When he asked Col. J, the Col. said, "Mrs. Miller came with me and Mrs. Miller will go home with me." I knew then that he would watch out for me.

During the time I was there, they had inspection teams come in from different places. One inspection team had been in Europe. They were in the middle of the Berlin Airlift, which went through Goose Bay, Labrador, on a stopover. Jack had told me about the officer's club there and how they redecorated it in this awful color, fuchsia. I asked one of the officers, "Have you seen the officer's club in Goose Bay, since it was painted fuchsia?"

He said, "Yes, I've been there and the color is totally out of place. On our way out of the Officers' Club, we saw a broken bust of someone in the lobby floor and a drunk person standing over it. His friends took the pieces outside and threw them in all directions in the snow to cover up the accident."

One day when Jack got home, we were talking about that Officer's Club. Jack was responsible for materials as well as other areas. He said, "One of the things I could never solve was what happened to the bust in the entryway of the officer's club. I was even held over to try and figure it out."

I said, "I know what happened to it!"

CHAPTER 12

Life in the Air Force

1948 (age 21)

I missed Jack terribly, while he was in Labrador. He wrote to me almost every day and I responded to every letter. To ease my loneliness, the vitality of Atlanta kept me busy. I visited the Atlanta Journal, where Jack's mother worked, Rich's Department Store and all the exciting shopping spots. I spent many hours walking around downtown Atlanta. I loved the tall buildings, the hustle and bustle of the traffic, pedestrians and cars, and the street-lined shops of every kind imaginable. I was never bored.

Nelle Hardy, one of my stewardess friends, was an Atlanta girl and I saw her often. The Atlanta Journal wrote an article about Jack and me in the Sunday edition. Nelle was from a prominent family in Atlanta and was included in that article in the Society Section of the paper.

Sometimes my time spent in the busy retail areas caused me to want things I could not afford. One day while "window shopping", I found a beautiful red coat. I wanted that coat so much, but it cost over $100, so I bought it on credit. That investment provided me with many years of enjoyment wearing that red coat. I practically lived in that coat in Washington, DC; until one day, the cleaners ruined it.

I was part of a family in Atlanta who took care of me like a daughter. One time when I had an awful cold, Jack's grandmother made me an old-fashioned mustard plaster and put it on my chest. While I was recuperating, I got a telegram from Jack.

It said, "I'm coming to the U.S. to ferry an airplane. Meet me at the Kimble Hotel."

I threw that plaster off and went down to Jack's mom's doctor. He gave me a breathing treatment and I went out to Eastern to catch a flight to meet Jack. In those days, the airport in Atlanta was so small that everyone knew everyone. I eagerly went to the Kimbrel Hotel in Massachusetts and waited, but Jack did not show up.

I saw one of the boys in Jack's unit in the lobby and asked, "Have you come from Goose Bay?"

He said, "Yes, I know that Jack is ferrying an airplane that's going to the airplane cemetery."

When you are in the military or a military spouse, you learn to be patient and flexible. Without question, I waited for him. He did finally show up and we spent two wonderful days together before he had to head back to Goose Bay and I went back to Atlanta.

Since I had been in Atlanta, I had depended on someone else or the trolley for my transportation, so we decided it was time to buy a car. Jack's stepfather was the Advertising Manager for the Atlanta Journal and had a lot of influence with car dealers around town. It was not easy to buy a car in those days. You had to get on a waiting list, but his stepfather arranged for us to get a little Ford coupe that had a visor on the outside front. It was originally supposed to go to the Coca Cola Company, but they released one for us.

The Air Force had extended Jack's deployment from twelve months to fourteen months. He did not get home until January 1949.

His next assignment was Keesler Air Force Base in Biloxi, Mississippi. Before we went to Biloxi, we took a short vacation back to West Palm Beach.

While we were there, I introduced Jack to Betty. She could not appreciate Jack's directness and they did not hit it off. She told me that she had heard some disturbing news about Doc and the condition of the property in Jensen Beach. I had not seen Betty in a while, and was glad to see her, but from the start, Betty was so different from me. I loved the outdoors and being one with nature. Betty clung to Mom and loved doing things in the house. I thought she was a pansy and not interesting. She developed into a successful businesswoman, but she and I never were able to be sisters. We were too different. Our goals, styles and priorities were too divergent to be close. I did not intend to ignore Betty's comments about Doc, but I did not have time or inclination on this trip to investigate because Jack and I had so little time together. I did not know that would turn out to be a huge mistake.

We also visited a friend of Jack's who had a Pomeranian ball of fluff that we fell in love with. His friend was trying to find a home for her because he transferred. We took her gladly and named her Miss Prissy. We took our little Ford and Miss Prissy to Biloxi, but it was hard to find a place to live. There was a horrible housing shortage. All the building supplies and construction labor were being used in the war.

We did find a two-room cottage by the lake, almost in town. It was across the street from the Gulf. It had a beautiful view and we were settling in as family of three. Since there were only two rooms, I did not have much to take care of and became bored easily. Miss Prissy was company for me while Jack worked. She followed me from room to room. If I sat, she jumped into my lap. I would take her on walks to the nearby park and look at houses along the street, wondering if we would live here long enough to buy a home that I could decorate.

We didn't have money to go out much, but we could go to the movies on the base. One night when Jack got home from a relatively easy day I said, "Honey, I'd love to go to a movie tonight. Do you feel up to it?"

"Sure. It's a perfect night for a date!"

When we got back from the movie, we found Miss Prissy in the kitchen next to the trashcan with her head in a small potato chip bag. She must have put her head in it for the salt. She had suffocated. She was such a joyous part of our days, wagging her tail when we came in the room, chasing her toys as we threw them across the room and jumping in our laps when we sat down. We were devastated!

As young newlyweds, we weren't being careful with how we spent our money, so we ran out of money often. The folks that lived next to us had the same problem. They improvised by making Brunswager sandwiches with tomatoes at the end of each month. They invited us over for those sandwiches several times.

We were constantly on the lookout for a better place to live. On the north end of the town heading toward Gulfport a woman had quite a few quaint cottages behind her beautiful home on the Gulf.

The cottages were not lovely like her house, but they were more than sufficient for our needs. When we saw a sign that one was empty, we immediately contacted her about it. We acted quickly and were lucky to rent one of those bungalows.

The "cottage" was of log construction. Military personnel rented four or five of these houses. We had quite a time in that little place.

This was the first place that felt like our home. It had one bedroom, with a living room, dining room, bath and kitchen, which had an old-fashioned stove. We lovingly called these cottages, slave quarters. It was a community of like people, in similar situations with little money and living at the beck-and-call of the military. We did not know how long we would be there, or where we would go next.

Good luck seemed to follow us. We never planned any of these choices; they just opened up for us.

CHAPTER 13

Not a Perfect Home

1949 (age 22)

We were so proud to have our own place. Jack wanted to be the man of the house and take care of maintenance of our new residence. He painted the bedroom and the dining room table as we settled in to our cottage. He warned, "If you shake the table real hard the leg will come off." We enjoyed our quirky life and laughed at this slight inconvenience.

Life was a daily surprise. Wild cats got on our screened porch. Jack was a sight to see when he put on work gloves and tried to catch them, but he could not, so he had to just run them off, which was another fiasco. Later, we got a little kitten that we called Puss.

The bathroom floor was uneven and rotted. We asked the owner to fix the floor before we moved in, but she only bought the tile for us to install. Jack planned to put the new floor down. They were cheap linoleum and flaked up when he installed a few of them, so we went over to Gulfport to buy new tiles. When we saw the price of new tiles, we decided that we didn't want to put our money into this place. We just lived with the floor the way it was.

After we had been there a while, we went to a formal occasion dance at the air base. We put on our best "bib and tucker" and left for the dance. We had to pass a house that sat back quite a ways off the road. It had the appearance of a nice big white house, but it was a gambling place. It was the only one in the area at that time.

As we rode by, Jack said, "Let's stop for a few minutes and check out this place."

Always up for an adventure, I said, "Okay that will be fun."

In the beginning, we were winning money. I was winning and Jack was winning. It was great, but we stayed too long because we lost everything we had….all our winnings, plus all the rest of our money.

That made us pretty poor. It was almost at the end of the month, so I went downtown for the first time, and the last time, to a pawnshop and pawned my little diamond watch to carry us until payday. As soon as we got a paycheck, I went back to the pawnshop and retrieved my watch.

We supplemented our food budget with fish from the river across the street. We dug worms and caught fish to have for our dinner. Military pay didn't stretch far so we had to be creative in ways to make ends meet.

We weren't in Biloxi very long. Then Jack got orders to go to communication school in Scott Field, Illinois. We had signed a rental agreement with the woman who owned the 'slave quarters'. She told Jack we could not have a rebate because we were leaving early. It did not make sense; there was a waiting list for her cottages because of the housing shortage.

I said, "Jack let me go try."

I went down to her house and I started crying, with big tears rolling down my face. She gave us the rebate. Sometimes, tears work really well, so off we went to Scott Field, Illinois, in our little Ford car with the cat, Puss, in the window.

We had to stay in a hotel for a few days while Jack oriented in his position there. I scanned the ads and found us a place to stay in O'Fallon. Illinois. Once again, that was quite a feat because of the housing shortage.

It was a two-room attic house and we had to go downstairs to use the bathroom, but the folks there were so good us. The landlord, Les Fowler, invited us to their 'Country Dinners' several times.

Every Saturday the men all got together and pitched horse shoes. Jack had so much fun. They had a little farm there too, with corn growing in the back. When we went to their house on Sunday to eat with them, there would be pork chops piled high on the table and several vegetables. In those days, everyone who had a spot of land planted a garden to help stretch the budget.

Les had a brother who was quite a character and lived across the street. You could hear country music coming from his house regularly, because he used to play country songs all the time. His favorite song was "Slipping Around, Afraid You Might Be Found."

Les's brother would go around the house to see what Les was growing, so he could have part of it for the winter. Jack told us that when they were pitching horseshoes, he would go into the garage and see a bunch of onions Les' brother had put up. When Jack came out of the garage he would say, "I see Les has onions."

They told us a story about a time when they were going to California. They were taking their grandmother with them in an old car. The car all packed with a mattress on the top allowing Grandmother to sit up in front. They looked like the Okey's heading out. Seeing them off, friends were making bets that they would not get past St. Louis. Well, they went all the way to California. Sometime later, they came back. Jack got a kick out of that. He loved a good story.

One day it got icy cold and we could not find Puss. We looked out the window and saw that she was trying to get in the basement of the house to get out of the cold. She had her head and one-half of her body inside and the other half (her tail) frozen like ice, but we defrosted her and she lived. Jack took her out to the base to have her neutered. He went to pick her up in a cardboard box. We put her on the floor and watched her flop around, until the sedation wore off. That was an interesting sight, but she was okay.

While we were there in O'Fallon, we befriended a couple named McTyre. The wife's name was Pamela and they had a baby named Linda. McTyre was originally from Atlanta. Pamela worked for Allan Foods, so I decided to get a job while we were there. I worked as a secretary for Allan Foods shipping department at age 22. What a time I had! That old fool I worked for chased me around the table more than once, but he never did catch me. Fending off bosses or other men in the company has always been a part of a woman's work life, when she works out of the home. It came with the territory.

I learned that there was only one other girl from the military base that worked at Allan Foods. She was from Canada, but she was in Goose bay, Labrador, the same time as Jack. She was the librarian there.

At Christmas, we went to Aunt Noni's in Springfield, Illinois. We had a wonderful time. I showed Jack where I went to school and where I stayed while I was up there.

CHAPTER 14

Life Outside
the Military

1950 (age 23)

Then in January of 1950, the Air Force had a big cut in personnel. They wiped out the communication school, which meant that Jack was out of the service during the year.

We went to West Palm Beach to live and after a few days staying with my mother, we found an apartment in North Palm Beach. On the way there I said, "I'm going to work on Worth Avenue in Palm Beach for Wagstaff & Bryant."

And I did! I was a secretary and I had a great time. I knew most of all the shop owners and heard a lot of gossip about the very rich, especially from the lingerie shop owners. Sometimes I ate a sandwich at the apothecary-restaurant down the street.

Jack went to work as a car salesman for Minner Motors. We moved down to the south end of town, past my mother's house, in a small bedroom/kitchenette apt until we could find a house.

Times were exciting down there, and some of the people were strange. One man had a pet tiger that he rode around town in the backseat of his convertible. Jack and I with some friends would sneak down to the river on the grassy area in front of the mansions and fish just for fun. The residents never caught us.

We located a house on Ridgeland Drive and purchased it. Jack was the leading salesman for Minner Motors and we won a couch and a rattan coffee table for the house. That was all the furniture we had when we started out. Later, we were able to buy a few other things.

Since we were living so close to my dad, we visited frequently and things between us became comfortable. It seemed that every time I saw Dad he talked about Doc and the Pitchford property. I really didn't want to hear about the infighting and problems with Doc. On this occasion, Dad was serious and concerned.

He said, "Let's go for a ride in my new boat."

I was excited about that, "Sure. That should be fun!"

As we got out on the river, he headed toward the Camp and the Big House. Dad waved his hand in a giant circle toward the shore and said, "Everybody thinks all of this belongs to us. But it doesn't."

I wasn't sure what he meant by that, but he wouldn't say anything else.

One weekend later, he invited me to come over to the Bahamas to the straw market.

I loved it and, impulsively, decided to go into business selling hats and bags in Palm Beach. Dad helped me pack up a gunnysack full of straw hats and bags. I brought them back to West Palm Beach. Back then, there were no customs.

Now, I had to decide how to market them. Therefore, I went to the Palm Beach Bank that had windows in front, where they displayed items for different stores every month. I asked them if I could have a window. They said one was coming available, so I rushed out to get items to fill the display window. Finding what I needed was easy because I already had in mind how the window would look. A fish company gave me a fish net for the background. Palm Beach Mercantile gave me some rush square for the floor bottom. The beach shop in the Palm Beach Biltmore Hotel gave me a background model.

I hung my hats and bags around the netting and put hand-written signs telling where to buy them. I also convinced the merchants on Worth Avenue to put the hats and bags in their shops on consignment. They became hot items, which meant I was going to Nassau in the Bahamas almost every weekend to get more hats and bags. A Palm Beach paper called 'Shiny Sheet' featured Lilly Ponds, walking down Worth Avenue wearing one of my hats, which was a huge boost to their popularity.

I took my lunch hour to collect my money and restock the stores. Food was not important when I could use my time to make money!

While Jack was at Minner Motors, he sold our car to have a down payment on the house on Ridgeland Avenue. Minner Motors provided him with a car, but we needed a car of our own. At age 23, I made enough money selling the straw hats and bags to buy a yellow Studebaker convertible. It wasn't new, but it was cute.

Later, we sold our house on Ridgeland Drive. We had just moved into our new house on Parker Avenue when Jack received orders. Jack had stayed a Reserve Officer in the military and the Air Force recalled him and assigned him to Eglin AFB for the next four years.

When those orders came, we rented the house on Parker Ave. My mother kept it rented for us over several years. We always liked to refer to it as our bank, because we refinanced it several times over those years. Every time we had a need for cash, we would refinance it, because it appraised for more than we owed.

The military never left us in one place very long. I really got accustomed to moving and seeing what life was like in different cities. Leaving West Palm again, we went up to Eglin Air Force Base on the panhandle of Florida. We were there four years and lived off base in a house. Then we moved a little closer to the base into another house. We had some unbelievable times there.

One time we looked out the window and saw the ugliest bulldog we had ever seen. She was pregnant and she belonged to a major who lived next door. When she had puppies, they were not thoroughbred bulldogs, so the Major gave us one. We named her Susie. Shortly after that, we got quarters on the base.

They were new L-shaped duplexes. We had great neighbors, including the Shaffers, Col. Bevins and his wife and Loren Allers. Loren helped Jack build a barbecue pit in the back yard. Every weekend they barbecued out there and all the neighbors came over. Later, Col. Bevins became a General in Washington and came to a party we had at the Mount Vernon Country Club.

In those days, military personnel had more than one job. Jack was the operations officer but he was also responsible for the pilot's club and the golf course too. One time, he had several errands to run. He went over to the club and then ran another errand to check the stock from the previous weekend at the Airmen's Club. Then he went downtown and was on his way back to the base. Homestead was the beach party property and the only paved road from the gulf to the base.

Back in the "primitive days", the cops wore dungarees with big red handkerchiefs hanging out of their pockets. They ran the roads and it seemed they made money every time they pulled somebody in. They pulled Jack in one time.

The cop said, "You crossed the centerline. Get out! You are drunk! We're taking you in." They made him leave the car at the side of the road and they took him to jail at Crestview.

When he got there, he had one call he could make and he called me and said, "I'm at Crestview. Come and get me."

There must have been dozens of people in uniforms in this big enclosure. So, they were making quite a bit of money off boys from the base. I walked up to Jack and I was as nervous as I could be because I did not know what had happened.

Jack said, "Hello there. Meet Dillinger." I will never forget that. I thought he was going to burst laughing. Because of Jack's connections, he was able to get this incident out of his records.

The other thing that happened while we were at Eglin was that Jack stopped at a place on the highway coming into town, and had a beer. He had the bulldog, Susie, with him.

A man came into the bar and said, "Whoever has that yellow convertible out there, better go on out, because the dog has eaten up the car." Jack went out to check and Susie had chewed all the leather seats up. He had to have all of them recovered.

I was fortunate that I always found a job everywhere we lived. At Eglin Air Force Base in Florida, I worked as a secretary. Eglin was a special assignment for us, because that is where I became pregnant with our first child. I was very pregnant.

CHAPTER 15

Children Complete the Family

1952 (age 25)

On August 18, 1952, at age 25, I gave birth to our first daughter, Marilyn Jean. Grandmother and husband Frank came a week before the due date to be there when the baby was born, but 'lo and behold' the due date arrived and she was not born. They stayed two weeks, took me through many bumpy rides, and gave me some castor oil. Finally, it was time and we went to the hospital for me to have the baby.

It was not a hospital. Converted Barracks housed delivery rooms for the babies. There were a couple of big doors leading to the delivery room, which was on the right; and the waiting room, the size of a bathroom, was on the left. As you went down the corridor, there were little booths with curtains around them. I did not deliver right away, so I spent quite a few hours walking up and down that corridor.

Way into the night a man and a woman came in with the woman screaming. Everybody rushed to help. They took her in immediately; she had the baby and was back in her cubicle by the next morning. She was a big German girl. The next morning she was walking around talking to all the girls, "Well, what can I do for you?" She said, "When you have babies you scream real loud and it doesn't hurt." We found out that this was her third baby.

Eglin Air Force Base was an important part of the Air Force. It was the proving ground for the climatic hanger. Jack was in charge of the Golf Course and Airman's Club besides taking flights.

I worked as a clerk-steno until I was eight months pregnant. We had so many great friends there. Jack and neighbor Capt. Loren Allers were popular for their all day weekend bar-b-ques on a large homemade pit in our back yard.

1954 (age 27)

Then Jack got orders to go to Korea, but deployment for Korea never happened. Marilyn contracted the measles while the movers were at the house packing. Jack got new orders from the base commander to put the furniture back. The Air Force reassigned him to Saudi Arabia.

The year Jack was in Saudi Arabia, I worked for the City of West Palm Beach in the Rec Dept. I was in charge of the playground and volunteered at Morrison AFB hospital. Once again, we had our life together put on hold for the military, and we were going to spend another year apart.

Jack was in the Rescue unit of the Air Force in Saudi Arabia. His excellent flying skills, positive attitude and love of flying made him a perfect fit for the job. He regularly made many open sea landings in SA-16 planes to rescue folks in all sorts of situations. He even took folks off burning ships. His was a special flying technique. He loved this job and used these skills after retirement when he was with the Shriners and flew burn victims in our private plane to a burn center in Greenville, South Carolina.

1955 (age 28)

After his assigned year in Saudi Arabia, Jack came home to Warner Robbins AFB in Georgia. This deployment had Jack's flights going south to the Islands. During the time we lived in Warner Robins, Jack was gone a lot and I played golf a lot.

While Jack was on one of his trips, I found better housing and moved us to the new house. I did not tell Jack, I just left a note on the first house with the address where I had moved us. I gave Jack another surprise!

CHAPTER 16

From Jensen Beach to Washington, DC

Late 1956 (age 29)

Our transfer from Warner Robbins, Georgia, to Washington, DC was a result of Jack being handpicked to fly SAM (Special Air Missions), during the Eisenhower administration.

SAM pilots flew the President's plane and other dignitaries in Air Force planes. This was a high honor and we were proud for him. In those days there were only about 30 pilots designated SAM. Jack was the pilot for Vice Presidents Richard Nixon and Lyndon B. Johnson. Vice President Johnson called Jack Capt. Jack and Vice President Nixon called him Jack Miller.

Jack blossomed during this time. He was in his element. He had the poise and personality for the job. In addition, his love for flying made this a dream job for him. He flew dignitaries from many countries all over the United States, showing them our beautiful country's mountains, deserts, rivers and major cities. Sometimes, he would be gone a couple of weeks at a time. He was "the pilot" for the dignitary for their entire visit.

1957 (age 30)

First, Jack's base was at Washington National Airport; then he moved to Boiling AFB in Maryland; then to Andrews AFB. Jack had many stories about the trips with these dignitaries and their wives, but someone else will have to tell these stories.

Some flights were memorable, not because of whom he flew or where he flew, but because of what happened when he landed at his destination. Once, Jack flew the Secretary of the Air Force to Fresno, California for the Veterans' Day Ceremony. When they got off the plane, Mom's brother, Uncle Britt, who was head of the Welcoming Committee for the Secretary of the Air Force, surprisingly greeted them.

Mom kept in touch with her younger brother on holidays, but as a family, we didn't see him. As a young man, he lived in Jensen with their parents, went into the Coast Guard, and became an officer. After the war, he went into the insurance business and met his wife, Mabel, in Syracuse, New York. Over the years, he had become quite successful as a leader in the community and, therefore, had the distinction and honor to welcome the Secretary of the Air Force to Fresno to lead the ceremony.

We knew a couple of the Presidential pilots: Jim Cross was Johnson's pilot and Jim Swindle was Kennedy's pilot and had flown him to Dallas, Texas, the day of the assassination. Jim said he never wanted to fly again, and retired shortly afterwards. Jack flew the Secret Service to Dallas the day before the assassination. He received a call the next day to go pick up a brain surgeon to operate on President Kennedy. Before he left, they called back and cancelled. They informed him that President Kennedy had died. Jack was at the office when the Hot Line called.

Some of Jack's flights were not political. He flew to New York to pick up dresses for Jackie Kennedy from Olge Cassini or to pick up a rocking chair she wanted. These trips took place in smaller planes. The Vice Presidential planes were smaller than the Presidents planes and these planes, which flew Congressmen and their wives, were smaller than the Vice Presidents planes.

I met Mamie Eisenhower at Pan American's christening of the first 707 jet. She came to our luncheon of about 30 girls. I sat with her and Juan Trippe, the owner of Pan American Airlines. Jack was in charge of the reception upstairs after the christening. Mamie complained about the heat in the room because she liked to be cool. Her aide told Jack he had to turn down the air conditioner for her in the reception room after the ceremony. He learned to accommodate every wish of the Presidents' families. The ladies group invited Mamie (as she liked to be called) to a luncheon. She graciously accepted and visited with us for a long time. I won a centerpiece at the luncheon and for sentimental reasons used it at Christmas for many years.

After retirement, we returned every three or four years to reunions of the SAM squad. The last ones enveloped a complete military wing. The Washington Airport had also grown so large we needed directions for how to get in and out of it. On one of our last trips, we visited Mt. Vernon Country Club, which had grown from a nine-hole course to an 18-hole course with the clubhouse doubled in size.

Our family was growing. Jacque was born July 1, 1957, in Alexandria, Virginia. I felt my waist was getting too big during my pregnancy. The Stauffer Reducing Coach was popular, so I went to see a demonstration. The manager took my order, and she immediately asked me to join the company, selling their units, so I went to work for Stauffer Reducing as a figure consultant. I was not looking for a job. This just fell in my lap.

Their product was a motorized platform that jiggled you while lying on it, to lose weight. I had great success with this business, since all the leads came to me. We found a full time black housekeeper named Nora, for the children. She drove a Caddy (Cadillac) and only worked for the love of it, not for the money.

I joined co-worker, Jackie Hanson, at fashion shows to demonstrate the machine at Andrews AFB and Fort Belvoir. We sold some to the Washington Police when they had a campaign to help officers lose weight and get healthy. I almost made it to SAC (Strategic Air Command) Ready Room in the Air Force for a demonstration, but later that year, someone wrote an article in the newspaper that the process did not work.

I was in the office when I read the article. That article killed sales and destroyed the company. I told a friend, "I'm going for a real estate career." Right then I went to see Routh Robbins and started in real estate. I had seen how much money real estate brokers made and felt I could be successful and have financial security in this profession. This idea had been germinating in my mind for a while. I believed that Real Estate could keep me challenged and enthusiastic about working.

CHAPTER 17

From Nickels to Millions

1958 (age 31)

I grew from one challenge to another, making my way. I thought about my first business, selling fish bait off the dock in Jensen Beach. Back then, I made nickels selling grunt bait to anglers and now I planned to make millions in real estate. My life had almost been a mystery. That angel on my shoulder did not give notice. She just showed up.

I was not much for school. Neither was I interested in girl talk. Nor was I a sexpot (except with Jack). I was a tomboy and well-liked in school. I was a Girl Scout, and I played the clarinet in my high school band. I was unpredictable, and one time I stuffed cotton in my clarinet during a concert.

From the start, I loved making money. Why? Was it in my genes? Was it the Pitchford drive? Or was it what I had learned from my dad? Sure, I loved what money could buy, but more than that, I loved the challenge of making the money.

I passed the Real Estate Exam on the first try. Then I went to work for Routh Robbins, the largest real estate company in Washington, DC at that time. I started very successful and became the top listing agent. I saved enough money to buy Springfield Realty with John Callio who had been the manager of Routh Robbins. John had the perfect personality for real estate. He also taught Dale Carnegie Courses. John said if he went to class unprepared, he would just talk about what Beverly did that day. He taught me the basics of real estate.

We opened an office together and before we got started with the new company, I sold lots for $4,000.00 commission. We hired seven agents in a short time and business was good, but I wanted to sell only land. I learned that large plots of land could make you more money and offered more challenges and creativity than selling individual homes.

Jack and I borrowed $500.00 from Mom to put a down payment on our first house there. It was a three-level town-house next to an elementary school, where Marilyn started first grade. With the first snow, the adults gathered garbage can lids and played outside with the kids sliding down the hill beside our townhouse.

I only sold land at that time. Irene Caldwell was my first property sale. That was quite a first, because I had to find a buyer who needed that property. Cecil Sills was on the board of a new bank. He was a builder and knew the owner of a restaurant that needed a new location. I convinced him to purchase the property and build a restaurant for Blackwelder, the restaurant owner. At the first board meeting, the only loan they voted on was to Cecil. The loan was unsecured, but Cecil built the restaurant and it was a huge success.

The challenge of this first deal got me more excited about the possibilities with real estate. Then I sold my share of the company to John and transferred to Art Post Real Estate, the leading realtor in land sales. Roz Silver also came to Art Post Real Estate. We did great things together. I was confident in my abilities after the two previous sales. However, there are difficulties in every endeavor.

I presented, what I thought was a good deal to some buyers in Washington, DC. They would not even consider my plan, because they were not accustomed to dealing with women. I failed. I cried all the way home. After I became experienced with putting deals together, I went back to them and closed on several properties.

I sold the Goth wait Farm that became the first development for Dulles Airport. With the commission, I bought a beautiful house on Curtis Avenue in Mt. Vernon, Virginia. Going from military housing to a country club was a dream. Beginning with the drive into the community, there was a feeling of success, a show of money and an atmosphere of calm and peace that I never felt before. The waves of emerald green lawns flowing from one yard to the next, divided by pristine driveways of rock, stone or brick highlighted the façade of the houses. Our home was a two- story brick structure with floor to ceiling windows on the golf course side. Black shutters flanked the windows on the front of the house. There were three bed-rooms, a formal dining room off the kitchen, which was open to the great room. The gourmet kitchen had a baker's island and an additional table in the nook. I could see myself working in the adjoining room as my office.

Jack and I were charter members of the Mt. Vernon Country Club. We, also, belonged to the Andrews AFB Golf Club and Fort Belvoir Golf Club. We loved golf and it was an excellent way to meet 'movers and shakers' who bought prop-erty to develop. We played golf several times a week. Jack and I both loved the game and always played together. We were both better than average golfers were and played in many compe-titions. Golfing brought us together in the midst of beautiful golf courses. It was our way of enjoying nature, even if it was developed and designed nature. At these events, we bonded over another activity that we were good at and brought us joy. We belonged to a Southern States group that we travelled with and enjoyed vacationing in beautiful cities around the South.

I was busy becoming successful in real estate and Jack was busy flying many VIP's of the world. Many times he would be with them a week, showing them the important places in our country. For the eight years that Jack had this assignment, he always went to work in full uniform, no fatigues. I loved seeing him in his uniform. He was proud to wear it.

Irene Caldwell had become a very dear friend. I never dreamed of being part of the elite in Washington, DC, but it happened naturally. Irene introduced us to the top social life of Washington. With her by my side, I became comfortable in the presence of important, powerful people. We even shared a box at the symphony with an ambassador across from the President. We went to the Symphony Ball, where we met the Conductor of the Symphony. Then we met Mrs. Merriweather Post, heir to the Post Cereal Company, who was Chairman of the event. Here I spent some time talking to President Eisenhower's neighbor from the Gettysburg Farm.

One time Irene invited us to party at the motion pictures headquarters, where Eric Johnson, President of the Motion Picture Industry, attended. There were influential people everywhere I looked. I even danced with Glenn Ford while Jack was in deep conversation with Yvette Mimieux. Pearle Mesta hosted the party that included Esther Coopersmith who was the up-and-coming 'Hostess with the Mostest' in Washington. Her husband, Jack, bought real estate from me. He owned dozens of fast food restaurants and gas stations, but worked out of a one-man tiny office, which had boxes stacked near to the ceiling of each of his properties. One time when I called him, he answered his phone in another country. That is the way he conducted business.

I spent Sunday afternoons at teas with the Press Club. The Secretary of the US Mint and many other important people showed up from time to time. These tea parties did not resemble tea parties in Jensen Beach.

Early in her life, Irene hosted large political parties. As we became friends, I helped with the planning of the parties. We engaged the head steward on the VIP aircraft where Jack worked to cater one of the parties. There were so many wealthy attendees at the party that Irene had a police officer at each door. Her apartment was lavish and perfect for these large parties. When she and her husband first moved to Washington, they lived in an apartment on the top floor of the Willard Hotel. Later, at a luncheon with Irene, I met Mrs. Marriott. She and her husband had married at Irene's Chicago apartment.

Irene had many friends in Washington. She supported many charities and made philanthropic contributions to healthcare, religious and educational institutions, which exemplified her giving nature. She was particularly interested in poverty in and around the Appalachians. Her special project included a whole section of Kentucky; she developed the land and took care of the folks who lived there. She had a small house in Virginia that she used to store packed food and supplies for these people. She sent the packages by rail. At one point, she went to see the folks who were receiving her support. She visited one house where a baby had just been born. As she approached the front of the house, she recognized the flattened boxes that held the supplies as insulation nailed on the house. Over the years, she kept up with this family, baby girl, and made sure the girl received a good education, including piano lessons. Years later, after my daughter, Marilyn, left for college, I sent several formals from her Rainbow coronations to that girl for her piano recitals.

Mrs. Caldwell adopted four orphaned children. She enrolled them in special schools and purchased 20 acres of land with a run-down stately house on it. She had the house jacked up and she and the boys worked on the house on the weekends.

The boys loved the work. Irene earmarked it for the boys when she died.

Our time in Washington was full of unexpected introductions and elegant parties. Sometimes I wanted to pinch myself to be sure I was not dreaming. At one charity event, I met Mrs. Eugene Rietzke who chaired the event at Marjorie Posts' Hillwood home where we toured her extensive flower gardens. Later Mrs. Rietzke invited us for dinner at her estate on the Potomac near the home of Jackie O's mother.

After a short time in Washington, Jack reached the rank of Major. The standard promotion events were stand-up cocktail parties, which were sometimes boring. In the middle of the night, I woke with an idea to have Jack's party on one of the large boats that floated down the Potomac. Jack liked the idea and so did the other promoted officers. The result was a party called the Binge on a Barge. It was a huge success.

CHAPTER 18

Living High

1968 (age 41)

By now, Jack and I were living well. We had a huge party at the Mt. Vernon Club—dinner and dance—we took over the whole club. My mom and step-dad, Frank Soper, came from West Palm Beach to the party. They were in the receiving line and Frank said, "I'm Soper," to Rex Pirkle. Rex said back to

Frank, "I'm drunk!" My friend, Jackie Henderson was Jackie
Pirkle then. Years later, Jackie told me that Rex told that story
many times.

I made so many great real estate deals from gravel pits to
the largest paint and body shop on the coastline. Cash Carlson
owned the junk yard. He became a special friend.

Success had a downside. Jack had sexual encounters a
few times, while on out-of- town trips. Men face the temptation to look for excitement and intrigue in someone outside of
the marriage as a challenge. Jack and I both had temptations.
Temptation is not the issue. Problems begin by giving in to the
temptation. At first, I had a "feeling" that something was not
right. Then I "knew" something was wrong.

Jack's encounters were one-night stands. He was one of
the boys, where drinking was the core of every get together.
The overindulgence caused unclear thinking and an attitude
that it is okay for men to "sow their oats". In a close culture people talk, but I never mentioned his indiscretions to him. They
hurt, but my marriage was more important to me than dealing
with the backlash of a conversation about his infidelity. I loved
Jack and I knew he loved me. Airing my knowledge about his
slips in judgment to him would only cause friction and a wall
between us that would always be there, or his guilt might cause
him to leave. I did not want a broken family like the one I had
as a teenager.

One night while he was away, I could not sleep and visual-
ized him with other women. I began to resent his philandering
until I realized that it could have happened to me too. I remembered some of the near misses I had while Jack was in Saudi
Arabia. I worked at the air base as a Gray Lady where I met a

sergeant whose son had been in a popular movie. We talked about the movie and became friends. One day he asked me for a date. I refused but I was so disappointed in him because he knew Jack and he knew we were married.

I guess military men approach wives of other military men because they know they are lonely while their husbands are overseas and might be looking for company. Once when I was at the dog races while Jack was still in Saudi Arabia, a couple of air force officers struck up a conversation with my friend and me.

One of the officers asked me, "Do you want to go to Palm Beach for a cocktail?"

Without thinking, I said, "Okay." We had a nice evening. There was nothing physical and I went home safely, but he asked, "Can I see you tomorrow?"

We saw each other the next day before he flew back to his base. I became nervous because we did have some chemistry then. He leaned in, kissed me goodbye, and slipped a note in my hand with his address. "Just in case you want to see me again."

I sent him a Christmas card and wrote on it that we moved to Warner Robins. A few months later he called, "Hi Bev, I'm in Warner Robins. Can you see me?"

I did want to see him, "Let's meet at the park in the middle of town at the lake. I can't wait to see you."

We had a good visit and I enjoyed talking with him, but I realized we were just friends. I am happy that I did not get involved with him, but it would have been so easy to continue the relationship.

Another time when I worked at Georgia Tech an Army officer who drove me to work each day asked if I would go to

Fort Bragg and spend the weekend with him. Again, I said "no", but was aghast and insulted.

Remembering these near misses made me realize how easy it could be to be unfaithful, but I am a one-man woman, and my one man was Jack.

CHAPTER 19

Jack Retires from the Military

1964 (Beverly age 37, Jack 41)

I started Ole Town Realty with Bruce Bass. I made one good sale before we left in September 1964.

While I was with Art Post, I became acquainted with the big boys in Washington and sold them many sites. I remember they all had lunch at the Ambassador at their "round table". They were all Jewish, except Allan Crowe and his brother Gerry. I sold Allan several sites and one night Gerry called me to say, "I just made my first million." Allan had reached that mark some time earlier.

I knew Allan had an eye for me, and I admired him. I almost gave in to my inclination, but I did not want to put myself into the situation that Jack had chosen. Allan called me one night to ask if I would meet him at one of his apartment houses in Maryland. I said yes, I would meet him, but I did not go. I almost went. I wanted to go, but I did not want to lose Jack's trust if he ever found out. Even though he had been unfaithful, my conscience would not let me break my vow to him. I will never know if Allan went.

Later Allan bought the estate Jackie Kennedy grew up in. He became a real estate giant in Orlando and everywhere around Washington.

When Jack retired from USAF in September 1964, we sold Curtis Avenue for a nice profit and left for West Palm Beach. Jack's Air Force career had ended. I hated to leave all the glamour and real estate deals. Before we left, I went to my friend, Roselyn, and laid out my last sale. She followed up with it and closed the deal. She made $40,000 commission and sent me 10% or $4,000, a gift.

1965 (Bev 38, Jack 42)

We retired to West Palm Beach and soon bought a house in Lake Clarke Shores, 8430 Pine Tree Lane. We built a swimming pool and bought a small boat for the Lake.

Marilyn started seventh grade and Jacque started second. Marilyn was learning to play the piano and when our furniture arrived we all sang to her playing, 'O Solo Mio'. Later we learned that our Jewish neighbors said, "Oh, my gosh. A bunch of Italians have moved in." We became very good friends with them. Their daughter, Pamela, and Jacque still stay in touch.

After a while in 1965, we realized our money was running low, so Jack started looking around for his next move. "I do not want to be 'that private pilot' who carries the luggage around for wealthy passengers," he declared. "I need a project, an opportunity."

Once again, God put us where we needed to be and provided for us with the unexpected. In Jack's search for a business, he became acquainted with Mr. and Mrs. W. H. Zander. Mr. Zander had just retired from Monarch Die and Engineering Corporation of Dayton, Ohio. He developed a product called SpenZal, which was a highly efficient plastic wall dispenser. It held toothpaste, hand cream, shampoo and other similar every day products that come in tubes. At that point, Mr. Zander had not done any marketing for it. Jack was impressed with the product and felt he could market it.

He met with Mr. Zander, "I would like to buy the manufacturing and distributing rights for the product and pay you a royalty." Mr. Zander wanted to be a part of the company and liked Jack's proposal. They quickly made a deal that pleased them both.

Jack placed an ad in a national salesmen's magazine with a picture of the dispenser and a description of how it functioned. This was the first marketing effort. Amazingly, we received thousands of orders from that ad. The success of the product continued through additional ads in other sales magazines and through our development of a training program for independent salesmen. Jack was making excellent marketing decisions and the company was growing. Next, we sold ads to several magazines and to Spencer Gifts.

An international network of independent salesmen and distributors quickly formed and in the second year, orders quadrupled. By the third, year sales had tripled again and resulted in us relocating the business into a modern building with extensive offices, warehouse and an assembly department and shipping department. Soon, we had distributors in all fifty states and in Canada, Latin America and Europe. SpenZal was going great and we were living well on the profits from the company.

Jack and I were so much alike in our approach to business and making money. He was not satisfied with just sitting back and living off SpenZal. He wanted to make something else successful. Jack was looking for a new challenge when he met the Morrison's. They had a new product that Jack felt would revolutionize painting. He contracted with them to manufacture a disposable Filler Paint Cup and financed Mr. Morrison's travels to tour the southern paint shops for orders. Jack ordered 100,000 special metal disposable cups from the Dixie Cup Company and hundreds of the metal paint fillers. We all thought this product would revolutionize painting and be a big success. However, no one tested the cups up-front. Having a positive gut feeling does not take the place of good research and product testing.

Sadly, the cups leaked and it was a total failure. Jack had to take a second mortgage on the Pine Tree house in West Palm to pay off the debt we accrued from this failure. This was another time that the Pine Tree house bailed us out of a bad situation.

While we were living in West Palm Beach, Betty came to visit occasionally. Once when she came to visit Mom she dropped by our house. I was busy cooking, so she went into Jack's home office to talk. He was at his lowest point with the failure of Filler Paint Cup and did not really feel like talking.

Betty saddled up to the desk. "Jack, how are things? Have you been to the RV Camp? Have you talked with Doc?"

Jack looked up at her and said, "I'm not interested in those issues."

Betty glared at him, whirled around and left our house without speaking to me. She did not talk to Jack for two years.

This was the lowest point in Jack's career. He felt like a total failure. He had never experienced failure before. He did not know how to handle it. Therefore, he started stopping by a local bar and drinking beer to pass the time. Alcohol took over his free time and caused a rift in our family life. One night on his way home, car lights from on-coming vehicles barreled toward him and blinded his vision. He was going down a street the wrong way. I believe God was in the car with him and directed Jack off that street safely. At that time, he was the Master of the Masonic Lodge and an incident like this would have marred his reputation if it became public. At home in our driveway, Jack sat in the car crying and made a decision that this was the end of his drinking. He called a neighbor who was in AA and he never took another drink of alcohol.

As a member of AA Jack helped several prominent men in the community join AA—our house builder and wife, several folks from Pratt & Whitney (an aerospace manufacturing company) and a local judge and his wife. They came to our house for meetings. We called ourselves the Cottage Group.

Involvement in AA brought my Jack out of his distressed time. Goodness filled his life again. He had a talent for talking with people and could bring out the best in them. Inviting people to AA meetings was easy for him. His experience made him realize how the program could benefit anyone who had a problem with an addiction. Many prominent men got help because of Jack. The lifestyle of social drinking that turned into daily drinking was pervasive during these years and caused many folks to develop a habit that they had never intended to create.

About this time, I had a yearning to get back into real estate. Jack's mom had retired from the Atlanta Journal and moved to nearby Lake Worth. She willingly took my place at SpenZal and looked forward to continue working. Helping us out made her feel a part of our lives, and allowed me to start Beverly Miller, Inc. Real Estate.

Through all the years of our marriage and the exciting life we lived, I did not think much about Dad or his life. Jack and I were moving up and out and my attention was on my family and career. The lessons Dad had taught me, as a child, were a part of my fiber. They inspired the way I handled myself and were the basis for my ability to make money. At this point in my life, I was not thinking about Dad's uncanny premonition that someday when I returned to Jensen Beach, I would need to rely on lessons he taught me about his brother, Doc, when he included me in every confrontation they had.

In all my disappointment, anger and shame about what Dad had done, I did not bother to look deep into the man who loved and raised me. I did not understand that he knew very well what his family's weaknesses were and had been preparing me for the job I would inherit one day.

CHAPTER 20

The End of an Era

1974 (Beverly age 47)

One day, I had an urge, no; it was an uncontrollable need to go visit my dad. I did not see him regularly, but we were on cordial terms. I felt a void in my life and knew that only Dad could fill. Jack was okay with me taking the trip alone.

I went to Dad's house in Jensen and surprised him. He was very happy to see me. We had dinner and talked for hours. I felt a strong family connection to the Pitchfords on that trip. Through all of our rough times, I always honored my dad, because he was my dad. I didn't have to agree with everything he did, but I did love and respect him for being my dad. He gave me such a great start in life by trusting me to do things that sometimes stretched my abilities. Those adventures caused me to grow, to believe in myself and to take safe chances. I was never a daredevil, but I did like to stretch the limits sometimes.

During our conversation, Dad shared with me, "Bev, after your mom and I divorced, I was at a very low point. I was lost. I realized I had messed up. I wrote to your mom several times, asking for forgiveness, but she had such high standards that she couldn't forgive me."

"Dad, you still had your mistress living with you!"

"I know, but I would have ended it, if Wanda had taken me back. I moved to Nassau. However, I didn't stay there much. I mostly sailed around the Bahamas in my 60-foot schooner, Ranger. In 1953, I also did some diving and in one cave found a treasure chest filled with gold coins. I haven't spent the gold. It's still in the chest, just like I found it."

That was the end of that conversation. I did not remind Dad that he had married his mistress and only divorced her after she cheated on him. It seemed that Dad was not sorry about their divorce. You couldn't tell what Dad felt.

Dad and I did not talk about the Pitchford property or any of his brothers, but he told me to use my business acumen when dealing with them, especially Doc. Dad protected his brothers and their name until his death. He did not admit to anyone that they wasted all the profits from the family and diminished respect for the 'Pitchford' name, resulting in the perceived curse that hovered over the family.

I wanted to ask him to explain his brothers' actions, but the visit was too important to me to tarnish it with talk about things we could not control or change, or so I thought at that time.

After a good visit reconnecting to my heritage, I wanted to get back to the present.

I remember those very last words to my dad.

"I have to go now. I have to go make some money."

He laughingly said, "Goodbye." That was just a few days before he died at age 71.

Dad must have known that his heart was about to give out. He and a friend went over to Cistern K and on the way back he stopped to see friends in West End. He was saying his goodbyes to everyone without them knowing it.

My father's funeral was huge. There were folks crammed into the church and out the front door. There was a lengthy write-up about him in the paper. Bill Pitchford, my dad, was an unusual man. He was different and interesting, adventurous and creative, unafraid to try new things.

Betty came to the funeral and we visited for a few minutes. "You know after you left Jensen Beach, Dad and I spent a lot of time together. You always said that you were like Dad and I was more like Mom. That was not true. Since you were out of the picture, he had time for me. We fished, took many excursions in his schooner, and met for lunch frequently. We became very close."

I was not shocked at this attitude toward me. "I'm sure you did, Betty. I am glad you had time with Dad. He was a remarkable man."

"You don't have to tell me that. You weren't around. You never gave him a chance after he and Mom divorced. He was still *our* Dad. People say I look more like him than you do."

Betty always stressed that he was our Dad; that he was part of her life too. "I never shunned him. I was just living my life, which happened to take me to places far from Jensen where I ran a very successful business."

"That doesn't mean that I haven't been successful. I am well known in Franklin, and during my years at the Chamber of Commerce, I have started many programs. "Pickin' on the Square", brings in hundreds of tourists, and the Scottish Museum housing the World's largest quilt is recognized in Washington, DC. I've built rental cottages for tourists and am recognized beyond Franklin as a creative business woman."

"No one is questioning your success, Betty. I am happy that you have found your calling and are happy. You are happy now, aren't you?"

"What a thing to ask someone," she glared at me as she turned and walked away. I didn't see her the rest of the day.

That was the typical attitude I got from Betty. I saw her as a frustrated woman with a huge chip on her shoulder. I was the target of her bitterness, especially when it came to Dad. This conversation was a distraction from my day. I was here to honor Dad and to be part of the celebration of his life. I dismissed further thoughts of Betty. At the end of the day, the outpouring of love and respect for Dad that so many people in and around Jensen showed overcame me.

Years before his death, Dad impulsively purchased a house on Cistern K Island in the Bahamas when he happened to stop there one day in his long-range schooner. He met the owners of the island, Darcy and Joy, and found out they were hard-up for money. Darcy and Joy bought the house and island property for $19,000, but the deal required him to stay on the island.

Darcy went to work for Senator Mailess. He would leave Joy on the island and go to work for the Senator during the week and on Friday, he would return with a week's worth of groceries. Dad said that Senator Mailess and Judge Sivan and Slim had an airplane and brought whisky in from the Bahamas.

The house Dad bought was on one side of a private runway with the ocean on the other side. Darcy and Joy planned to build houses on the island for tourists to rent. Tourism was beginning to flourish in the islands and they planned for this investment to be their livelihood. They had hired the natives as construction workers to build the houses and had started construction on a few. It had not panned out that way. They had lost their financing when the natives took over the islands from the English.

The native construction workers had used the house Dad bought, because it was the only house on the island beside the owners' house. There were some unfinished house frames, but they were uninhabitable.

I initially went back to Nassau to try to find out how my dad died. The owner met me and I expected him to take me to the house on Cistern K after we had lunch, but he said that I must go alone because he had work to do. He took me to a plane that would take me to Great Harbor where I would then catch a boat to take me to Cistern K. However, the plane was a little late, so I had to run down to the docks to catch another boat, which was leaving at five p.m.

I barely made it. I was the only passenger on a small boat with a huge native man. It was a little daunting for me to be in a boat out in the ocean with this man, but we made it to Cistern K, where Darcy's wife, Joy, was waiting and waving for me on the shore. I spent an informative night with her, listening to her animated stories, which included all the details of my dad's life on the island, but not his death. It seemed to be a mystery to her too.

I also found out that Marjorie had not only inherited Lot 6 which held the home Mom and Dad built in the Pitchford Subdivision, but had inherited the treasure chest with the gold coins in it. She gave it to her daughter, Rosemary, who later donated the chest to the Stuart Heritage Museum, minus the gold coins.

Six years later, Darcy and Joy notified me that they wanted to buy my dad's house. Jack and I had only been there one time before. At that time, the dopers were bad and in some areas, the hotels looked almost abandoned. We checked into customs at Great Harbor and coming in to land in Cistern K, we saw a wrecked plane under the water. The place was like a ghost town. We needed food and asked if there was any place to eat. The pilot directed us to a thatched roof hut on the beach. The only other people there were two gold-laden natives. We walked down the beach with our shoes in our hands. It took a while to reach the thatched roof structure and then even longer to get our cheese sandwiches, the only item on the menu.

When we flew to Cistern K from Great Harbor, Darcy and Joy said that they would never sell to the dopers, but Jack noticed that the shrubs were cut way back so big planes could land. To see the island in that condition made me sad and depressed. So, on the way back to West Palm I said, "Jack, let's stop on the way home and enjoy this trip."

Without reservations, we checked into the Freeport Hotel. We got a room, but it was less than desirable. I was so tired and dejected that I decided to take a bubble bath. When I slipped into the suds, I jumped right back out because there were two or three inches of red sand in the bottom of the tub under the suds. I wanted to make the best of the trip as we always did, and said, "Now that I've had my sand bath, let's go downstairs to dinner!"

Jack's sweet answer was, "I always wondered what you would feel like sanded down!" He laughed, grabbed my arm and we went downstairs to a great floorshow and dinner.

We traveled a lot and knew that things would sometimes go wrong and the trip might not be what we had expected. We learned early on to just enjoy whatever we could out of the trip and to limit our expectations.

The final trip to Cistern K was to close the deal for selling Dad's house to Darcy and Joy. They wanted to buy it back for $20,000, which was what Dad paid for it. We agreed to that amount and Jack flew over and picked up Darcy who had $20,000 cash in a suitcase. They flew back to our Pitchford lawyer's office to count the money. I think we guessed correctly that…the dopers must have moved in.

This was the most unusual and unlikely sale I ever made.

CHAPTER 21

Real Estate Won't Let Go of Me

1975 - 1977 (ages 48-50)
Beverly Miller Real Estate

At age 48, I had an overpowering desire to open my own real estate office. I had been successful selling real estate from the beginning, but I felt I could do so much more owning my own office. I knew I could make more money and have control over what deals I chose to work on. It was almost as if I had no choice about it. I was going to do this.

As I think about it now, that drive directed me all my life, starting with Dad's imprint on me. I saw it as the Pitchford way. As a young girl, I saw my uncles as innovators, business people, and in control. That is what I wanted, but why?

The Pitchford men started out as successful, hardworking and creative. Along the way, they gave up and became parasites. Why? I vowed that I would not turn out like that. I would not give up. Success and money proved family value. I was determined to remain successful. Making a lot of money would prove that the Pitchford name was not a disgrace!

Jack and I had been through tough times, but we never gave up. We knew we could be successful if we just kept working at it. I would not give up as my uncles had.

I opened my office, renting space from another real estate company. My real estate office phone number was 1776, the year of the Declaration of Independence. Someone asked me how I got that number. I said, "I asked for it."

Sometimes, it is just that simple. You just need to ask.

When I started my company, a good friend of mine from Washington, DC, Roz and her husband Stan, decided to move to Palm Beach. After a few months, they realized that they missed the Washington life and Alexandria, Virginia. Roz came by the office and left me a note that read,

"Dearest Bev-
Thanks for everything.

May this dollar
Be the start of your first million!"
(She left a dollar bill in the envelope)

And it was! This move was the beginning of my most successful real estate business. Over the years, I attended classes in real estate in Alabama on selling farmland and took other courses in Miami. I was one of the first graduates of the Florida Graduate Realtors Institute (GRI).

We were busy as a family, too. Marilyn was always a good student and was active in Rainbow Girls. Jack joined the Masons, Shriners Flying Fleet and other business clubs. We lived well during these years and were able to buy Marilyn a little convertible to start college in Tallahassee after her two years at Palm Beach Junior College. Jacque was into horses and showing dogs. She was a licensed dog handler. Life was good.

Colleagues thought of me as professional and aloof, mainly because I was a loner. The Big Boys in town rumored that the Chicago Mafia backed my company. In those days, women were not supposed to be jostling with the men in business deals. Some powerful men had to downplay a woman's success by trying to attribute it to some outside help, like the Mafia, sex with a colleague, or blackmail. They could not accept that a woman could manage high-level negotiations or plan a profitable development without a man's help. Many times, women had to endure "accidental" touching, vulgar talk or jokes about themselves between men, when they could hear the conversations. I refused to give in to any of that fodder.

The first day I walked into my office after I had it redesigned, I stood there taking it all in. It was so beautiful, that it took my breath away. My eyes roamed over the vital records maps on the walls and I tenderly touched the books from the County on the bookcase. At first, I rented desk space from a so-called real estate 'big shot', but he left soon after I arrived and sold me his records and furniture. As soon as he moved his personal belongings out, I started making the place my own. I replaced old brass lamps with white ceramic round lamps placed on a mahogany sofa table under the window overlooking Military Trail. I chose a mother-of-pearl lamp for my desk. I replaced the brown rug with a cream and yellow floral carpet. The brown leather sofa and chair would do for a while, until I made some big money. I yanked down the heavy, smoke-drenched drapes and replaced them with white cotton curtains.

My office on 1000 Military Trail was only a little over a mile from our new house on Cleary Road, so I had a special telephone line run from my office to my home, so I would never miss an important call. Jack said that he would have never imagined anyone else closing big money deals in her nightgown.

After he sold SpenZal, Jack took real estate courses and got his real estate brokers license. His first sale was a large apartment complex. He did other things like managing condominium rentals in Wellington for a Canadian doctor and selling the apartment house in North Palm Beach. He stayed busy doing errands, etc. In addition, at home he raised special turkeys and fighting chickens that he did not use for fighting. His original mom and pop chickens grew into about two hundred birds. They had nests everywhere, above the stalls in the barn, in the woodpile, etc. Our friends would say, "Jack Miller lives where those chickens are."

One day when I was out riding around looking for property, I decided to look for that mansion property that I loved years before, but I couldn't find it. There was a wall where I remembered the mansion, but I could not see the structure. The owner was a Willis Jeep heir, but she became part of another wealthy family in her second marriage.

She told me the way she met her second husband was remarkable. She was in Washington, DC, walking down the street. Mr. Lawrence happened to be walking behind her and saw a person who looked suspicious following her, so he continued to follow her too. Just before the robber approached her, Mr. Lawrence grabbed her arm and saved her from the man.

That was the start of their romance. They married and lived in the mansion, but as she got older and frail, she could not negotiate stairs. Therefore, Mr. Lawrence had the top floor of the mansion demolished and enlarged the ground level to the same square footage. Part of that renovation consisted of leveling the grounds and building a wall to protect the property and provide privacy. That is why I couldn't find it when I looked for it earlier.

The owner was the Willis Jeep heir. A couple of years earlier I had called her in hopes of listing the property and she said, "Oh, no. We're going to raise tomatoes."

This jewel of a property was the beginning of a big future for me. The next time I approached her, she insisted she could not offer the property for sale, because it was a tree farm. Then, I wrote her and her husband a letter that convinced them to open this property up for sale.

I sold the property to the Mobil Oil Company for $11,000,000 cash. The Mobil Oil Company developed it into

River Bridge Community with over 500 acres consisting of 4,000 houses and 40 acres of commercial property on both sides of Jog Road. The total acreage went from river to ocean. The property had to meet several contingencies to make the deal work.

I received a personal check from her for $500,000. She lived in the second largest Palm Beach property that ran from the ocean to the river and was one block from Mira Largo.

Years later when we were living in Melbourne, I had the habit of looking on-line for money that was held to be dispersed to rightful heirs and found that she had never touched the money from the sale to the Mobil Oil Company. Her husband told Jack that he took all that money and bought Alaskan Pipeline stock. The stock was averaging eighteen percent in 1989. I could not believe it. When he died I guess he never told her about the $11,000,000, which had grown to a very large amount.

There was a common practice for folks who dealt in real estate to find money for heirs that they either, did not know they had, or had forgotten about it. For a commission, they would act as the heir's broker to handle all the paperwork to get the forgotten money back to them. I wanted to contact the family and let them know that money was out there and I could handle the paperwork, but Jack would not let me make the call. Sometime later, I saw where someone else had done just that. I considered that easy commission money lost for me.

I loved going into my office each day. It had an atmosphere of energy, with a design of class and calm. In the beginning, I did not use a receptionist, but I had a reception area. The walls between my office and the reception area were glass. I could see anyone coming or going, but that activity did not disturb me. It was the perfect place for me to research, design, make contacts and create deals.

Putting deals together was my specialty. I teamed up with an engineering firm, Rossi-Malavasi and a builder to create a development combining seven properties. My part was to contract with all seven, and I did. Malavasi did all the engineering and a builder was the buyer of all seven properties. The three of us pulled the whole thing off and sold it to a developer who built a subdivision called Sabal Palms.

I liked to use my money to help folks. I had loaned Diane $5,000 to buy merchandise for her new dress shop in Stuart. She and I went back a long way. Diane's sister had a flower shop in Seneca, South Carolina, and I knew her when we lived in Keowee Key, SC. It seemed magical how friendships and relationships from one place that I lived turned up in another place and generally worked into a sale or purchase of real estate. I felt silently guided from above.

Once again, I just happened to be at the airport one day when a private jet landed with Kenny Sims deplaning. I said, "Kenny, the last time I saw you was in a steak house in Virginia. You said you had just come in from flying lessons."

He said, "Yeah, it's been a while. I'm here because I have a hotel in Palm Beach, The Vinita, that I want to sell." The hotel was less than two blocks from Worth Avenue. I got to work and sold the hotel in less than two weeks. The worst part of the deal was that Jack and I had to inventory all the rooms on all three floors, plus the restaurant.

Kenny was one of a kind. He chartered Elizabeth Taylor around to spas and other vacation places. He also owned several nursing homes and many other businesses. He had a home on the water in Palm Beach and a castle in West Virginia.

My first large sale was to a Baptist Church on Jog Road. I found a perfect eight acres, but the church only wanted five acres. I was not going to lose this sale, so, I agreed to buy the other three acres. We called our property Millers Pines. We got county approval to create Palm Beach's smallest Planned Unit Development (PUD) on the records.

Over time, I made a ton of money, selling over 1,000 total acres of prime property. I sold a junkyard lot for the largest paint and body manufacturer, International Harvester, in Virginia.

Again, it just felt right. We were Sustaining Members of the Palm Beach Round Table, which was a professional club that brought in speakers from all around the United States. We were active in our community and were active in our church, leading the youth group for a couple of years. I was happy making money, but somewhere in the back of my mind, I felt that I would use the money for good, for something bigger than myself.

At this time, Jack and I had purchased our beloved airplane with the commission from the Sabal Palms sale. Jack and I made friends with the Mobile Oil Executive, Jim, and his wife, Judy. We traveled everywhere in our plane with them: Key West, Bahamas, South Carolina, Franklin, etc. We kept up with them over the years and had lunch with them when they visited their daughter in Atlanta in 2015.

I purchased a 20- acre corner of Jog and Summit Boulevard along with a rich partner in Palm Beach who paid half of the contract and advanced $60,000 for sewer connections. I did all the zoning changes, PUD plans through the county, obtained lift station permits, etc. and I named our 112-townhouse development, Parkside Green. I prepared the property for building, but I did not want to build and sell the houses. Therefore, I sold it to Felix Perez. We made about $600,000 and kept out five acres on a corner for future sales. We later sold the five acres for $50,000 each.

In addition, I hit big again with the Sandy Loam properties owned by Madam Chereau, a very wealthy lady from France who owned a perfume company and several medical firms. She had poor vision, so she gave the properties to her grandsons, who lived mostly in Switzerland. The first deal we made was to Coronet Development who built Abbey Park, a townhouse development of several hundred units on the south side of the Famel Property. My sales girl, Virginia P. was also private secretary to Madam Chereau. Madam Chereau grandsons were contract sellers. Because they were not U.S. citizens, they had to close the deal outside of the United States, which caused me to charter a twin-engine plane for a flight to the Bahamas for the closing.

Next, I sold Felix Perez several hundred acres of valuable development property he called Summit Pines. At first, Mr. Perez tried to go around me when he was planning to buy Lily Demetri,'s (Earl Flynn's wife) property, which would give him more acreage at the Chereau property. He had his son try to take the sale away from me and give it to his real estate friends in Palm Beach. I beat him to the punch and sold it to Bob Long before Mr. Perez could buy it. He was in shock when I told him. When I ran into Mr. Perez' secretary, I told her that he was tough.

She said, "You tough too!" That day I won his respect and lasting friendship. I will never forget the look on his face when I told him that I had sold the property to Bob Long, who developed it.

Things were hopping in real estate at that time. I worked many long hours, but I loved it. Our home needed to keep running too, so Jack and I hired a housekeeper/nanny for the girls. This move was a lifesaver for me. Even though I missed the girls, I never regretted the decision. I knew that they were safe and well-taken care of so that I could concentrate on my work and build a financial future for the family.

Thinking ahead for my next sale, I purchased five acres with a sizeable house that had an oversized living room with a fireplace that I hoped Felix Perez could add to the Parkside Green PUD development. I had my engineer friend look at it and he said that the house would not qualify as a clubhouse. However, Mr. Perez was able to pull off the deal and made a great clubhouse out of that property. He also built two-story rentals on the Forest Hill property I sold to him.

I did many more sales with Felix Perez. When he learned about Jack's flying background he wanted Jack to fly him to his various developments. Jack liked him and it was a fun time for him. Jack flew him regularly around Florida to his bustling warehouse developments. They chartered twin-engine planes because Mr. Perez would not fly in a single engine plane.

Once you start in a business, the contacts you make go with you the rest of your career. If there are good results, you most likely will have future success with them. If the results are not good, you will have to work harder the next time, if you get a next time. I had good relationships with my clients and we each made money from my proposals. I was fair to them and expected them to be fair to me. In the end, everyone was happy and richer.

However, there are dirty dealings in real estate as in any other business. I met with Sam Dresden when he and his wife were in the area and noticed my sign. He called me and asked if he could come by the office to talk. It was like 'old home week'. Sam did site planning for companies I had worked with in Virginia. He did not have any money, but he knew a group in Miami who might go for a deal he wanted to make with a 105-acre corner property at Lake Worth Road and Route 7. The Miami group came to view the property. They asked us to come to Miami to talk sale. Jack and I flew to Miami and they met with Sam first. He came out of the meeting and said they had cut him out of the deal.

I said, "Okay, Sam. Let's go for it my way." He moved to West Palm Beach from Miami. He was successful working with the county for rezoning, and permits. He loved the feeling of being in charge. Virginia and I split all of Sam Dresden's expenses during the time he spent getting the property rezoned.

My plan worked this way. The original price of the 105 acres was $800,000. I sold it to a rich Palm Beach friend. She lived on the top floor in the best apartments on Worth Avenue. It had a swimming pool on the roof outside her apartment. She had married the two wealthiest men in St. Louis, Missouri before moving to West Palm Beach. When the first husband died, she married the other one.

Then, I re-sold the 105 acres for $1,200,000 (on paper) to Sam Dresden, giving my friend a $400,000 profit. The next sale was to Dr. Birch, a South American client, for $1,500,000.

He had an office in Miami surrounded by a guarded wall. We named it Woods Walk. It became a luxury development! All three contracts closed at the same time. I had commissions on all three pieces of property and split my profit with my agent friend who worked with the Famel grandsons. Surprisingly, Sam Dresden had his own attorney at the closing and tried to cut me out of the deal, even though I had included him when the Miami group wanted to cut him out. I had planned to share our profit and my real estate commission with him.

Therefore, my answer to that move was, "You can't do that. Sam's contract has expired". I thought he would faint.

The attorney's remark was, "What else are you going to pull out of that briefcase?"

Real estate closings for all the above transactions were a circus and when Dr. Birch shook my hand, I felt like he almost broke it.

This was a perfect example of control. You have to protect yourself when making large financial deals like this. I had the same control with all of the Perez deals. I stayed one-step ahead of him on every project we collaborated on, and we remained friends.

The result was a beautiful subdivision called Woods Walk with over 100 lots in an upscale subdivision with a 20-acre corner zoned commercial.

When we flew down to Miami that day, the Tower announced…"Hold up Pan American for Fr 24-J to land." That was our plane. I felt very important that day in our new airplane.

I knew about the availability of the property across the street from the Mobile Oil tract, which was also across the street from my friend. We teamed up to develop this land. I promised her a big profit in two to three years. I had heard about a development in Ormond Beach that I thought would be perfect for our property. Therefore, I flew to Ormond Beach to look at that development. I copied the plans for it and we used it to develop our property.

Looking at my record book, I sold twelve developments in a ten-mile radius. At times, I was showing the result of too much work! I was frequently tired and lost interest in most everything except work.

After Jack retired, I sold River Bridge, Summit Pines, Summit Apartments, Abby Park, Woods Walk and Sabal Palms, which altogether amounted to about ten big and small developments.

One day I was sweeping pine needles off the roof of our house on Cleary Road and saw a little girl go by on Jacque's first horse, Socky. That scene reminded me of a slower time in our family, one where we went to horse shows with Jacque and shared with Marilyn her successes in school. We had time to visit with each other, cook meals together, relax on weekends and just enjoy each other's company.

I got down from the roof and said, "Jack, it is time to go. When I saw Socky with another new owner, I realized that we have met our goal. The girls are both married and we are millionaires. Let's get on to our next adventure."

My friend, Roz's wish and dollar bill had inspired me to make it come true.

Jack grabbed me with a big hug and said, "Let's go!"

In two weeks, we sold out and went to Keowee Key. Jack drove a big mover that we called Yellow Bird and I drove our new Cady called Blue Bird. We kept up with our cbS3 license fun.

You have to know when to quit. When we left West Palm, we had a nice nest egg of about $1,000,000 in the bank and planned to retire to Keowee Key and play golf every day.

CHAPTER 22

Retirement Bliss

1978 (age Bev 51, Jack 56)

One day, sometime in 1978, I said to Jack, "I think it would be fun to ride in one of those big newer Air Force planes. Every Wednesday one leaves out of Patrick Air Force Base enroute to Africa with a stop in Antiqua." We did everything spontaneously, so we called Patrick AFB for the details and the next

Wednesday we found ourselves on a giant plane. We sat in this enclosed plane with no visible windows. There were some chairs strapped down in the center and the only thing in front of us was a load of freight. We ate lunch out of a little box that also had a bottle of water.

I said, "Jack, where is the pilot?"

Jack replied, "Up above."

I turned to see their lights two stories above us!

We were in Antiqua in a short time. We had a dream three-days there. First, we taxied all around to choose a hotel. We found a lush resort with a white sandy beach and breath-taking orange sunsets. It was close to shops where we walked each night. We had to meet the plane Saturday afternoon on its way back to the states from Africa. Jack called these adventures, "more honeymoon".

Later in 1979, we took another fun trip to San Juan, Puerto Rico. For a short time, while Pan American was negotiating with another airline to merge, they offered all ex-employees some unbelievable fares. Ours was $59 round trip. We left out of Miami and I thought it would be neat to stay in the same hotel I stayed in when I was with Pan Am. Luckily, we got a room at the renovated Normandy Hotel. It was walking distance to all the ole-time sites. It looked like a ship, and by the front desk, there was an elevator, which was smaller than the ones guests used to get to their rooms. Years back when I was there with Pan Am, I asked our crew captain where that elevator went and he replied, "Oh that goes to ill repute."

After that comment, I shut up! This time with Jack, I asked the front desk where that elevator went. The answer was, "Another restaurant!" Question finally answered.

After we made the rounds there, I said, "Let's take a ride on the native bus." We rode the bus to the other end of the island with the driver racing through some very tight places. Despite what I had told the Pan American recruiter when I applied for a job, we did not speak Spanish or we would have asked him to slow down. We had dinner at a beautiful hotel restaurant. Sparkling chandeliers hung low in the center of the room and the huge table under it had lavish vases of multi-colored island flowers. This was another honeymoon for sure.

We were still honeymooning for our 60th Anniversary. We flew from Atlanta to Hawaii and stayed in the military Hale Koa Hotel for a week. A friend of ours from Melbourne taught at the university there every summer. He took us around the island and we had a wonderful time dining at a large luau. The cast called us on stage and they prompted Jack to sing the Hawaiian love song to me. Jack had a beautiful voice. In school, he was in the glee club and sang in a quartet in high school.

We took another get-away honeymoon trip to California, Mexico, back to California and up the coast stopping at various interesting places. We stayed at two brand new hotels and were the first to occupy the rooms where we stayed. We saw Capistrano (where the birds come back every year) and then went to Palm Springs. On the way there, we passed the miles of windmills used to produce electricity. Next stop, Los Angeles and then back to Atlanta. Everything was first class.

We, also, went to every Sam Fox Reunion ever held. Sam Fox is a special air missions unit for the President and any important visitors to the United States like Ambassadors. These men flew the influential folks around the US and showed them our National Treasures. We saw the unit grow from thirty people to hundreds over the years. Once we went to a Washington hotel dinner by bus and I noticed Jim and Emily Swindle in the very back of the bus. Jim had flown President Kennedy. I thought, "What a shame that the President's pilot had to sit in the back of the bus!"

We drove out to see our Curtis Avenue house. What a disappointment, the area had changed so much. Our house had a huge patio out back where we often entertained our neighbors. Additionally, we had an extra lot in back where we kept caged chickens, a rabbit hutch, and two ducks called Daffy and Daisy. When we retired, we took Daffy and Daisy to live with other ducks in view of the White House in Washington.

Still on the move, we left Stuart enroute to the Heritage Festival at Hilton Head, South Carolina. When we were in north Florida, we were flying not far above a smooth blanket of very white clouds. We were at 4,000 feet and I was bursting with pride. At one point, I thought how fortunate I was. I was such a long way from Pitchford's fishing dock and grunts. It was such a romantic feeling when I glanced over at Jack and saw from the smile on his face that his thoughts were not much different from mine. I imagined that smile was a replica of his smile as a little boy sitting behind the fan, pretending to fly a plane full of Washington VIP's.

One time we were on the way to Keowee Key from West Palm Beach where we had conducted some business. We were eager to get back home. When we got to Savannah the bad weather had moved in, so we went to our favorite hotel for the night. We had no luggage, so I bought an oversized mans t-shirt in the gift shop and slept in it and washed undies every night. We weathered in for three days, but we had fun. We ate at our favorite oyster house every night. It was so easy for us to make the best of every situation. We were both fun loving and enjoyed being together wherever we were.

Then there was the time we took our accountant and his wife to New Orleans. Felix Raw Oyster Bar was our favorite place to eat oysters, so we took Sidney and Joanne there as the first stop of the night. The spiced dip sauce was very, very hot. Joanne dipped too much hot sauce and followed it with beer. She could hardly speak. After dinner, Jack and I crashed at the hotel, while Joanne and Sidney enjoyed the nightlife in New Orleans.

In West Palm and Stuart, Florida, we joined a half-dozen other flying Shriners with planes for breakfast flights. I think we hit every airport in Florida. We all met at the Ramadi Ranch, a resort in south Florida, for overnight. The Orlando beer franchise owner for south Florida was there with his new million dollar Queen Air plane.

During the time that Jack was President of the Flying Shriners, we went to a ranch in northern Florida that had an airstrip, a lodge, and girls' rodeo every Friday night. The gift shop owner had placed a boot in the display window with a sign, "This is for a one-leg man." Our attorney friend only had one leg from his college days when he was turning a prop on an airplane. He decided to try the boot on, and it fit! Therefore, he wore it the rest of the trip.

We had yearly Shriner get-togethers in Jacksonville, Greenville, Memphis, Louisville, West Palm Beach, Nashville and Myrtle Beach. Each would last several days for meetings, banquets and games the guys played by flying their planes and dropping flour sacks on the ground to see who would be next to hit the target.

We were still having honeymoons into our 80's.

CHAPTER 23

Our Airplane Life

1980 (Bev 53, Jack 58)

Jack and I shared the exhilarating thrill and joy of flying and we were always thankful that flight was an important part of our lives, his as a pilot and mine as a stewardess and then passenger. It was another reminder that our lives connected us as soulmates.

We decided to buy our first plane in 1949. It crashed on a 100 hour-inspection flight.   Jack had already become an expert pilot in the Air Force, remaining cool and collected when something went wrong. He proved this on the inspection flight when something caused the solenoid on the plane to falter. The inspection mechanic was in the left seat for the flight. He headed the plane over some trees to try to make a landing on a golf course.

Jack told me, "I knew that the plane would never make it to the golf course, so I grabbed the controls and made a 180 degree turn to avoid them. Unfortunately, the plane made a crash landing anyway." Thankfully, both pilots were in good shape.

Someone called me right after the crash, "Your toy is all wrecked, but your husband is okay." I thanked the Man Upstairs for that.

We bought our second plane (24 Juliet) in 1980, which brought us another new life for 12 years. Jack studied lots of models and decided on another Piper Dakota because of its bigger, more powerful engines. We could carry the weight of four large people and a full baggage department. We went all out for instruments, so we could fly by instruments anywhere. The only thing we did not buy was a storm scope. At this time, Jack was chartering twin-engine planes to take, our real estate customer, Mr. Perez places. He bought us the best storm scope available, which cost over $10,000, so that Jack could use our plane for his charters rather than renting planes.

Our 24-J was then complete. We had $50,000 in instruments.

After we retired from the Air Force and moved to Cleary Road, I was on the way to the grocery store and had to pass by a dog track. It just so happened that dogs ran on Saturday after-noon. Almost without thinking, I turned into the dog venue, placed a bet and won $100. I promptly left after that win. I had learned my lesson about gambling when Jack and I lost all our money that night at the white house casino in Biloxi, early in Jack's career.

Then on the way home, I saw a sign on the airport that said, 'Learn to fly for $100.' I turned in there and said, "I want to fly."

The instructor said, "Let's go up and see how you make out."

It was a very windy day. We bounced around in the trainer, but I loved it. When we landed, I agreed to come back for les-sons. However, before I could return, the pilot had a heart attack and died in the Bahamas.

I did start lessons in West Palm Beach because our plane was more complemented than a trainer. I did not get licensed because I did not want to solo. Even though I spent most of my life going with my gut, or with God's guidance, making deci-sions on the spot, I was not a daredevil and I felt insecure about piloting a plane with other people in it. However, I did take two pinch-hitter courses to learn what to do in case something happened to Jack while we were in flight. Then I took lessons from an instructor from South Carolina. We flew to Sebastian Airport and I made about 10 landings on another windy day.

When we landed, Jack said to my instructor, "*I would have had a hard time landing in that wind.*" That made me feel better.

Jack was active in the Masons and Shriners and even participated in the Eastern Star. During those years, his pilot's license and our planes offered him a unique opportunity to help the community. When he was in Labrador, he did many rescue missions for folks who were in dangerous situations and got them to safety. Here, he donated many flights taking children to burn centers. That was special to families who needed to get their child to treatment quickly.

"I feel like I'm paying it forward to the next generation with these flights," Jack often said.

His trips to the Shriner Burn Center in Greenville, South Carolina, showed him the area where we eventually bought our lake home in Keowee Key, an upscale community with an 18-hole golf course and a first-class restaurant, large enough for tournament parties.

His involvement with the Eastern Star again showed his compassion for people. The reigning Eastern Star Worthy Matron's husband died. Part of her duties included having a man help with presenting parts of the program. Jack volunteered to be the Worthy Patron in these meetings. He had a photographic memory and within a few days could recite all the required statements without any help. She told him that she was so grateful to him for making her rein professional and fun.

1979-1983 (Beverly age 52, Jack 57)

Our life was full of airplanes, horses, boats and dogs.

Our first house in West Palm Beach was on Pine Tree Lane on a lake and had a swimming pool. I sold it for a profit and had a house built on Cleary Road with a barn and three acres. During the construction of the house, Jack spent nights in our motorhome on the property because thieves would steal everything they could find. Jack kept our Great Dane, Baron, and a little terrier with him. The terrier would sense if anyone came on the property and would alert Baron who circled the property and would send out a "woof" that scared anyone away.

The property had a chain link fence all around it with gates for the barn on two sides and gates fronting the house and a canal on one side. We had a telephone on a tree for use when we were outside working.

One late night they all awoke with a huge bark and then a scream. A couple of drunks had crashed their car and taken one side of the rail off. Jack immediately called the police. They asked, "Where are you calling from?"

Jack said, "From a tree."

After much laughter and consternation, the police arrived and arrested the drunks.

Jacque showed a love of horses and got us heavily involved showing and raising horses. Her first horse was a grade horse. Jacque had been doing well with the trainer, so we proceeded to find a horse for her. We found a nice looking gelding with white feet that she named Socky. Socky arrived at the trainer's barn, but the next morning when Jacque ran out to see him, he had broken out of the barn. He turned up a couple of miles away. Jacque began showing Socky a good bit and advanced to the next level. We admired the Eternal son's breed so we bought the Eternal Son Tag. However, before the big show at Gold Coast in January, Tag developed a bog leg. Therefore, Jacque could not ride him. Harold Howard's family, owners of the Eternal Son sire, was at the show and learned about Tag. They felt horrible about Tag's leg and invited Jacque to their farm in Michigan for the summer.

Just before Jacque was due to return home, she called Jack, "Daddy, Daddy, there is a wonderful two-year-old Eternal horse here, and her name is Jackie."

Jack could not disappoint Jacque. Therefore, we bought the horse, Jackie, and then had to figure out how to bring her home. Jack had never driven a horse trailer on a trip of this distance from Michigan to Florida. It turned out to be a complicated process, but with the help of Mr. Howard scheduling stops at other horse farms along the way, we made it home with Jackie safely.

Later, Jacque became interested in showing dogs because it was easier to transport them to shows.

Jack spent his time on the land. We had a dog, cats, and fighting chickens that we did not use for fighting. We had the Eastern Star picnic there for three years.

There was room for tables, tents, plenty of seating and lots of food. Our setting made the event fun for members. Some folks just spent time looking at the lake under the shade of one of our mature oak trees. Others rode in the boat or skied behind the boat. And some sat on the dock sun bathing, while the children swam in the cool water of the pool.

1983 (age 55)

We bought a condominium in Mill Creek Country Club, Franklin, N.C. as a summerhouse. Initially we went back and forth from our Stuart Condo to Keowee Key. Then we built a house in Jensen Beach.

Marilyn left after college. She went to Memphis for her masters and doctorate degrees. Then, Jacque and Bill married. Since we were 'empty nesters', we sold the horses one by one and moved to Keowee Key, South Carolina. We lived in an 'Active Lifestyle Community' on Lake Keowee. The community had a golf course, a club and a top-notch restaurant.

We spent many relaxing weekends inhaling the fresh South Carolina air and losing ourselves in the enticing ebb and flow of the lake water lapping the shoreline. The speedboats created the swell of waves with their tow of energetic skiers. Duke Energy built Lake Keowee in the 1970's to provide power to the Carolinas, as well as offer recreational opportunities for residents and visitors. Its 300 miles of shoreline highlighted mounds of individual islands throughout the lake. Its crystal azure water invites swimming and boating. The community we moved into was a peaceful respite for us after our years of moving, traveling and working hard. It was a haven for us and allowed us to get back to the social life we had enjoyed so much during our marriage.

We also kept a condominium in Stuart, Fl. We flew back and forth in our plane many times. We often took Keowee Key friends to the Islands and to Savannah for lunch. We were living well then.

We joined other planes while in West Palm Beach every Sunday for breakfast flights. We made almost every airport in Florida, several to Key West and a couple to Nassau.

It was a very special feeling sitting up in the sky, just the two of us. I would glance over at Jack and silently say to myself, "I am so happy to love Jack like I do."

On one of our flights heading back to Keowee Key, we had just left Stuart and before we reached Melbourne, we got a loud call, "24J, Vector West, Now." Just as we turned, a big rocket went off at Patrick Air Force Base and we had a front row unbe-lievable view. I will never forget that.

Somehow, everything we did had a romantic feel to it. We were on a 68-year honeymoon (with a little work included).

CHAPTER 24

North Carolina Vacation Home

1983 (Beverly age 55)

When we bought the condominium in Mill Creek Country Club, Franklin, N.C. as a summerhouse, it was the perfect getaway from hectic times in real estate. We went back and forth from the Stuart Condo to Keowee Key for several years. Then we built a house in Jensen Beach.

1985 (Beverly age 57) to 1993(age 63)

When we retired to Keowee Key, we sold the West Palm Beach house on Cleary Road but kept our condo in Stuart, Fl. Keowee Key was always fun times. We had a beautiful new float boat for lake sports, and we golfed with groups several times a week, enjoying the friends we made there. John and Teresa Ballew, who had become good friends, took a trip to Stuart, Florida to visit us in our condo. We were flying lots of places then and John and Teresa enjoyed a trip to the Bahamas with us.

Our Gainesville, Georgia, children visited often and Jackie's husband, Bill, was the best angler. We had our St. Charles daughter and family along with the Gainesville group there one Christmas. It just so happened to be the coldest Christmas, ever…down to five degrees at one point. Our grandson, Jack, had a toy car. He would run inside to charge it and then run out to drive it. He did this all afternoon.

These years were our first retirement years. However, I was keeping the Jensen family property afloat, after Dad died in 1974. I paid the taxes and tried to keep the scavengers away.

I, also, tried to keep up with Herb and Doc, but I would have had to live in Jensen to know everything that was going on there. I felt that my life was with *my* family, but I tried to do as much as Dad had done for his brothers. Part of me felt that, at some point, they needed to be responsible for themselves.

Somewhere in the back of my mind, I remembered that Doc had claimed control of all the Pitchford property, assuring that he and Margarete would have everything in their name, outside of the family Trust.

1986

Mom and Frank vacationed in North Carolina and eventually bought a cottage there. Later Frank passed away from an aggressive form of cancer. Mom passed away in 1986 after living many happy years with Frank.

CHAPTER 25

Hiccup to Retirement

1993 (age 66)

Then a call came from the Manager of Martin County that I needed to come down there and take over the 17-acre Pitchford property. Doc Pitchford was not paying the bills.

At the same time, we had just gotten a bad health report on Jack on his last flight physical. These events encouraged us to sell our wonderful airplane, after 12 great years in the air. Soon, we departed to Jensen Beach.

Things there were much worse than we had imagined.

1994-2004 (age 67 – 77)
The toughest years of my life.

We knew that we would have to take over the property at some point. For several years before we left West Palm Beach, I had paid the real estate taxes on all the Pitchford property, which ran about $40,000 a year. I thought I was doing all I could to keep track of the property, but all the years we traveled with the Air Force and lived in Virginia and North Carolina and in West Palm Beach, I didn't go back to check on my grandfather's legacy.

Grandfather Pitchford had previously taken care of all the debts on the property, but as he aged, he turned over the business side of the inheritance to Doc, who was the only son he trusted. Grandfather died in 1959, which left many years for Doc to gradually gain control of the Pitchford fortune.

Doc married Margarete and they lived in a house on the property. Doc had taken charge of Grandfather Pitchford's property, but he and Margarete wanted control of the entire property, which at one point was over four hundred acres. However, over the years Grandfather Pitchford had sold off various pieces to pay the bills because no one was working or bringing in any money. An attorney friend of mine purchased one piece of the property and later resold it for a profit large enough to send his two sons to college.

Now, I realized why every time Dad had a showdown meeting with his brother, Doc, he would take me with him. After Dad died, I took responsibility for overseeing what I could of the Jensen Beach properties. I did not know that Doc was, in essence, blackmailing Jay to stay around to help him, by saying that he was going to split all the proceeds with Jay when he finally got control of everything. Jay was scared to leave the premises because he did not want to lose his half of the proceeds. This obsession caused his divorce.

If it had not been for Uncle Blount, who owned the camp and the Pitchford Subdivision that he developed, there would be no property left. Uncle Blount had put all his property into a life estate for Grandfather and then to Grandfather's six sons. Nevertheless, the property ruled the brothers' lives. They sat around and waited for Grandfather Joe to die so that they could inherit the property and money and be "rich". They had given up on any dream that they had in their youth. They greedily waited for a windfall from Grandfather Pitchford to make their lives perfect. They had no idea how much debt each piece of property had or how much loss in value the property had absorbed because of neglect.

Doc's greed became a disease. He refused to use any of the money to help his siblings. His wife no longer lived on the property with him. She moved into a house in Stuart because she did not like Jensen Beach. Doc would visit her at night, but return the next morning to guard his inheritance.

She sat alone watching a black and white television in Stuart. Finally, she was so weak Doc would take a protein supplement for her to drink to keep her alive as long as he could. He felt that none of the property belonged to Herb, Joe, Tom,

Allan or Dad. Hording it absorbed his whole life. He even stole from the rest of the family. He had somehow managed to get brothers, Tom and Joe, to sign over their share of the inheritance to him. Trying to get Allan's son, Jay, to sign over his share, he told Jay that he was going to take over all the fortune and that he would share with him. Jay became so frustrated with Doc's badgering that he finally even refused to see Doc.

After Grandfather Pitchford died, Doc sold or gave away all of Grandmother's furniture, even after several of us told him we wanted a piece or two to remember Grandmother. As soon as he learned that someone in the family wanted an item that belonged to her, he would hide it, sell it or move it.

Doc must have thought of himself as a Robin Hood figure. He stole from the family to give to vultures who used him. He had a way of saying to strangers or new acquaintances, "This looks like you. And I want you to have it."

I found out that there is a man living near Fort Pierce, who claims to have a complete room from Doc's gifts. He has Great, Great, Grandfather's Civil War doctor's bag with instruments and the family gun case with wonderful old guns in it. There is still a plantation called Long Branch in Warrenton, North Carolina, that was his family's plantation. His part of the Pitchford family was successful and hard working. His grandfather educated all his sons and even named one Wake, for Wake Forest University.

Doc's thought process and motivation is shown by one useless routine that tells the story about the boats. The Pitchfords had purchased hundreds of small boats over the years. Rather than sell them and use the money to improve the dock, pier or grounds, he piled them up in various ditches around the property. Over time, puddled rain had rusted places in the bottoms of the ill-stored boats. Therefore, Doc had a seven-day schedule to go from ditch to ditch and pump out the water from the boats. I could not believe the wrong thinking in this project.

This is the type of issue I faced when I arrived in Jensen Beach.

A close friend of ours who worked at the Title Company always drew up notes and securities for us and dealt with Doc. She thought he was one of the old timers of the family and, therefore, had legal control of the property. Doc even put a piece of property in her name and I had to return it to the Trust I had formed.

Allan, the youngest of the sons, went in the Navy after college. When he left the Navy, he married his high school sweetheart. They had two children (Kathy and Jay), but Allan did not work after a short time when he returned home. For a while, he did work at Bill's Place while my dad was still there. After Grandfather was gone, he got a job as bridge-tender on the Stuart Bridge. Then he spent his time "fun" fishing and "cast-netting". He was not always dependent on Grandfather for a living, but he did not try to build a career either. He was afraid to get too far from the inheritance. His wife had enough of his disinterest in working and about a year before he died she divorced him. He was only in his 50's.

Doc and Herb sat in the camp office all day.

Joe left Jensen Beach and had a great job on the USS Hydrographer. He sent us gifts from different ports all over the world. We never knew why he came back to Jensen. When he returned, he ran Bill's Place until he got cancer on his face. He was acknowledged as the best looking of the Pitchford men, so when the cancer disfigured his face, Joe would not go out in public. Doc was running the show and did not take Joe to the hospital because they had no insurance or Medicare. Eventually, Doc and Herb did take him to the hospital in West Palm Beach. I went to see him and it was so sad to see the way he looked. I found a dermatologist to treat him, but it was too late. He died in the hospital.

When Jack and I got back to the RV Park, the shock of the mammoth disrepair astounded us. There was trash all over the grounds, squatters were living in some of the trailers, Doc was holdup in the big house and it was falling apart.

The first thing I did was to set up a meeting with attorneys to draw up a trust, which included my sister, Betty, Allen's children, Jay and Kathy and me. I am the oldest child of the oldest brother, so I took over the job of straightening out this mess. The day of the meeting, I noticed all the heirs (children and grandchildren) gathered in the parking lot outside of the lawyer's office. They all glared at me as I walked toward the door. They hired an accountant to attend the Trust meetings. After a couple of meetings, he told them that I was doing a great job and they did not need him, because what I was doing would benefit them.

At one of the Trust meetings, I learned that Doc had deeded his long time attorney almost half of the property with no written agreement. Therefore, I needed to get rid of him as the attorney. This was Doc's final blow to the family. Once again, Doc proved how two-faced he was. He wanted everything and did not want the family to have anything. He was always working behind the family's back.

About that time, Willard Harris, a cousin from North Carolina visited us. He retired as Comptroller of a large company, so I knew he would know how to handle this situation. I asked him to Co-Trust with me. Willard and I visited an attorney in North Carolina at his vacation home. We drove up with briefcases in hand and with deeds giving titles back to the Pitchford's Trust.

Sometime later, the attorney in Jensen told me, "I knew you had it made when you got Willard on board." Years later, we found a $10,000 check from the attorney's escrow account that had not been cashed.

In the beginning, I had to deal with Doc. Somehow, over the years, he was able to get Grandfather Pitchford's trust, and after Grandfather died, Doc was in control. I could not believe that he let his brothers, Tom and Joe, die without medical attention. Greed had wrapped itself around his heart and squeezed all goodness out. It blackened his thoughts and hardened his soul.

Herb was in bad shape with cancer when I got back to Jensen. The last time I had seen him was a few years earlier when I took him to the doctor, who had told him to stop on the way home and get a test for cancer. Herb blew it off with, "I'm not stopping. Doc will take care of me." Doc did not.

In order to get Herb to the doctor this time, I had to back the car up to the back door just to get him out of the house. I took him to a doctor for an operation, but it was too late. The cancer had spread. I moved him into one of the updated trailers and hired two sisters to take care of him day and night, until he passed away.

Doc also needed medical care. The first doctor we saw had to cut off his long underwear; he was so filthy. He said he could not help him and referred me to a dermatologist. The dermatologist diagnosed him with many large cancers, but referred us to a cardiologist. The cardiologist came out and told me that Doc's artery was ninety-nine percent closed and he needed an operation. Some of my advance checks from sales took care of those bills because Doc had no insurance.

Doc was too sick to deal with the RV Campground. The bank had refused to cash any more checks for him because every payment was delinquent. He told me," I've gone as far as I can go." Therefore, he willingly went with me to the lawyer's office and signed over all the property to the Family Trust.

He needed a social security number and did not know how to get one. I took him to Fort Pierce to apply. When the Social Security agent asked him his occupation he said, "I'm a fisherman."

I had him operated on twice. I negotiated with the hospital on the bill. While I was in the hospital with Doc, I reminisced about the time I lived near that hospital when I was a little girl. I tied my horse up to a tree next to the river in front of that hospital during classes at school. That tree was still standing. This was the time I saw the Seminole woman and began our conversation about Jack Tommy.

Besides the RV Park, there were an additional four acres for the Big House (Periwinkle), along with three vacant apartments and two old houses. Allan's wife lived in another house on the Church Street side. The back portion, called the bone yard, housed a big assortment of junk.

There was also a second three-acre lot with an old house located on the Savannah. That property had fresh water running from north to south about a mile inland from the rest of the properties and was on the Indian River.

The third piece of property was a 17-acre, partly developed, old trailer park owned by Herb, Tom and Joe. Herb deeded his share to Doc before he died. Tom and Joe had deeded their share earlier, which meant that Doc held legal title to all of the 17 acres.

To muddy the water even further, there was a man who appeared with a mortgage for about $125,000 on the three acres at the foot of Jensen Beach that included a "pour over" clause stating he could move into other property. I found a creative way to pay him off and get him out of the property battle.

Getting all the property clear of debt, I had to write 60 checks from our own bank account that totaled $46,000. Other issues to clear up titles were to take care of the violations issued by the county for property overgrowth and junk on the river shore. The money I had advanced to restore the property was repaid to me as the business grew.

Early one morning as I sat on the grassy knoll overlooking the Indian River, 'My River', I tried to understand how we had gotten here. This beautiful childhood place had been like a dream to me. Today it was a nightmare.

The Pitchford dynasty had developed the area into a notable property. The Pitchford brothers worked hard and made it a place of which to be proud. When I left to work at Pan Am, I never looked back. I expected the property to be here as I had left it, or maybe even better. When we saw how our beautiful Cleary Drive property deteriorated a few years after we sold it, I should have realized that the same thing could be happening to our property in Jensen. Dad did his best to hold things together, but after his death, it was as if the others did not care about this place anymore. They had drained it dry and left it to slowly deteriorate into a dump.

I was standing there, looking at that mess, and wondering how I would take care of it all, when I noticed a young man operating a large machine with a big lift. I asked him if he could help me with clearing rubble off the river shore. He did, and that was a beautiful day of relief for me!

He used his lift to load many dozens of trash piles that were lying around on the shore. The project took many weeks. We worked well together, cleaned up the place and became good friends.

Sometime later, his mother became our office manager. So many times in my life, things just came together, and this was one of the most helpful. God was always there!

We sold our condominium and beautiful Float Boat in Keowee Key and moved into the Stuart Condo. We later built a house on Skyline Drive on a lot I had paid $35,000 to cover real estate taxes, which were overdue for the RV Park property.

The clean-up work began. The building that had been the grocery store was on the riverfront side. The filling station (now a restaurant) with the upstairs apartment where mom and her family lived when she and Dad first met was also there. That building held a special meaning for me. The worst change to me was that the store was a second-hand junk store run by a man named Tiny.

Doc financed Tiny to buy 'stuff' for the store and split any profit from a sale. It did not work that way, because Doc would buy back most of the junk and store it in the run-down cabins. As a result, most of the 30 cabins contained nothing valuable.

The camp had some regulars and a few full-timers, but I had no idea how much money the rentals made, because Doc operated out of his shirt pocket. He had a maintenance man living on the west side but I did not know what Doc collected from that rent. The Pitchfords had a warehouse on the property nearby with twelve old refrigerators running at all times. This was more of Tiny's shenanigans.

Dad's brother, Herb had thirteen Volkswagens that he had collected as a hobby and he had driven each one around the camp to keep them running. Herb was somewhat restricted in his thinking because he had a plate in his head since he was in college at Georgia Southern. He and several other boys climbed onto the roof of a building to get a better view of a fight between two college boys when the roof collapsed. Herb almost died.

I evicted Tiny, had the building treated for termites and rented the building for a restaurant. The new tenant asked if her builder-husband could renovate it. I said, "Of course." The renovation turned out better than I could have expected. When I looked at it, I remembered the way it looked when I was a little girl. The couple stayed there for several years.

Next, I found Willie Cook, a black man who had a big truck with a boom attached. He demolished seventeen trailers and carried the debris to the junk yard. That left the problem of broken glass everywhere. I called in the labor force that I had hired to help clean up the grounds to rake up all the glass. I bought several big rakes. If I turned my head away from the workers, they would stop working and rest. I worked hard those few days.

It seemed that the Pitchford laziness had even penetrated hired workers!

Then I tackled a house abandoned for fifty years, where my sister's second husband lived as a child. We called it the Gideon house. Willie took the house to the dump also. I took chances and did not go to the county for permits for this work.

Later, I had a demo company take down a two-story house, another larger one story and most of the thirty cottages. In talking with the owner of the demo company, I learned that he had taken down a huge tower in Virginia. I remembered that I watched them demolish that tower, when I was part of the real sale on the brickyard in Virginia.

It is a small world.

The electrical system in the camp was a disaster. One night, I received a called in the rain to take care of a situation where sparks were flying on top of the trailers. An old man who lived by the main road conducted the only maintenance for the property. He was on vacation at that time. If I called a legitimate electric company, the county would shut us down. Willie Cook gave me the name of an electric company who came to help. The owner of Hurley Electric Company and I became good friends. His company wound up putting all new underground lines for 114 units over several months, because I did not have money to do it all at once.

Of course, there were problems with the sewer treatment plant installed many years ago when the county required it. The Plant Inspector who serviced it had $20,000 worth of notes that Doc had signed. Doc had told him to put the cost of servicing it on my account. He did not because he had been expecting to get ownership of some of the property by foreclosing the note he held that had 18% interest attached. His system ran, but it only worked for five toilets. The rest were on septic tanks. I lucked into a way to pay him off.

I had my real estate sign on another piece of property on the east side of the bridge that had the $125,000 mortgage on it. A man from Miami just happened by and saw my sign. He could not wait to buy it. He thought he had found a gold mine. He paid me cash immediately. With that money, I paid the mortgage in full, and paid the plant inspector. Unfortunately, for the buyer, the property became unbuildable because of mangroves. There again, another big problem was solved for me.

These times are hard for me to imagine now. I had the 'freeloaders' and 'good old boys' evicted, not through regular channels, but by force. One young man was living in an old SUV on the property. I tried being nice to get him to move, but he wouldn't, so I wound up putting dead fish in his car and then had it towed to the grave yard.

There was another person living in a mobile camper with broken windows and the air conditioning running full force-- at our expense because he was hooked up to the camp electricity. He cussed me out and I did the same to him. He knew darned well I meant it.

We had fixed up one of the houses next to the big house and rented it for a couple of years. After that time, it was vacant. One day I saw a bicycle in the yard and discovered a drifter had broken in and had been living in it. When I went inside, I found that he was gone but he had left a note that said, "I enjoyed living in the house".

There were other small incidents, like the time when things were really picking up, a motor home was moving out for the day and fell into a septic tank hole under the ground that no one knew was there. The owner's wife started yelling. It was Sunday and I had a tough time getting a load of sand and a wrecker to get the motor home out of the cavernous hole.

Jack was right there with me during these years. During all of our married life, we shared the good and the bad. We were there for each other and our love remained strong.

On December 17, 2004, on my 76th birthday Jack gave me the sweetest card. It said,

"Beverly—you have lived an exciting and wonderful life so far.
Now it is time to record all those years.
How great this story is going to be.
I have been lucky to have been a part
Of the last fifty-seven.
Please take the time to tell all!
Don't leave out anything.
This final chapter is going to be one of the best yet! We all love you and have a happy birthday.
        My Love,
        Jack"

Then the rebuilding began.

CHAPTER 26

Working our way out of Jensen Beach

1994 (age 67)

It took me ten years to clean up the Pitchford property and rebuild it back to its former glory. The curse that had trapped the Pitchford men had died with them. I prayed that my clean-up and repair work, and selling the property to responsible people would restore the Pitchford's reputation. I hoped the new owners would renew the original dream of Grandpa Pitchford's family, when they moved to Florida to build their future and make their fortune. Greed can destroy incentive in some folks. Instead of taking what they already have and making it improved, they sat back and rotted away in the filth of their greed.

I finally understood why my uncles lived the way they did. Each one of them had gone to college, except my dad and Allan, and Dad was the most successful of all the brothers. The greed for the family fortune drained the rest of them of energy and the desire to make their father's investment grow. Greed permeated the minds and lives of the brothers. They were afraid that leaving the property to go out on their own would endanger their share of the inheritance. They buried their treasure instead of investing it. It sounds like a parable in the Bible.

The thing that helped me the most with the rebuilding undertaking was what I had learned in Washington, DC from the 14th and K-street buyers about how to use Zoning and Site Planning effectively to make more money. In Palm Beach County, I used those skills.

The run down Pitchford property was the largest challenge of my life! I had to become "that tough lady" who kicked ass with trailer trash. I spent $100,000 or more to get the Park back to a viable RV Park. I used all the earnings from these properties for the improvements.

I felt that I should use the money I had made over the years here. My calling was to rebuild my family's reputation and respect, to value the land that was the starting place for each of us with the Pitchford name, and to honor Grandfather Pitchford. Money is only a commodity to use. I wanted the money I had earned used for good. For rebuilding. For future. For beauty.

I made sure everything was done correctly, including zoning. I started by demolishing 30 cottages and 5 houses and remaking the park with new electricity, water and sewer lines, fixing the railroad crossing arms and bells, redeveloping 16 new lots and making everything beautiful and inviting again. The result…I sold the property for $6,500,000.

Besides the 17-acre park property, I had grandfather's house (and about 5 acres) to deal with. Doc was living there amidst all the clutter. It looked like, no it actually was, the home of a hoarder. He fought me every step of the way, until I finally convinced him to let me fix the place up so we could make some money.

I bought Doc a golf cart with all his tools on it so he could ride around the Park. One day he was coming down the road into the Park and the cart got away from him, spilling all his tools as he tried to dodge the trailers on the dirt road. He could not control the golf cart. Someone finally yelled, "Turn the key off. Turn the key off." He was not supposed to leave the park grounds. He was a hardheaded man.

He had a girlfriend when he was 92, when I first got back to the property. I do not know that she qualified as a girlfriend; she was more like a leech. She was using Doc to get free rent. He said she was a nurse at the hospital, but in reality, she was in the housekeeping department at the hospital.

Early on, I saw that a young, sexy tenant was hanging around Doc way too much. As I questioned him about her, he said, "Well, she doesn't have the money to pay rent every month. So I let her skip a few payments now and then."

I watched for a few days and Doc would disappear overnight and appear the next day with her on his arm. One day I saw her walking from Doc's house, so I stopped her.

"Hi. I'm Beverly."

"I know who you are. Doc told me all about you. You're trying to evict all of us from our homes. You should be ashamed of yourself." She flung the words at me as she turned to walk away.

I followed behind her. "That's not true," I lied. "I'm just trying to update the records for tax purposes. How much is your rent each month?"

She stopped and glared at me, "You'll have to talk with Doc about my rent." And with that, she turned and pranced toward her trailer in her yellow bikini that barely covered any part of her body. She was tanned, shapely, and very confident about her status at the Camp. I decided that I would change that status.

The next time I saw her, I said, "I need to collect your rent." She took a long draw from her cigarette and did not take her eyes off me. She stomped off with no response. When I never received a payment from her, I went to her door, "You need to move out because the trailer is going to be repossessed."

She told Doc. He was furious with me. The next day, the repo company came and hooked up to the trailer. As they started out of the camp, Doc ran behind them yelling, "I've got the money! I've got the money!" They did not stop.

Another renter at the camp had seen her coming out of her trailer one morning, hanging all over a man who worked with her at the hospital, and told Doc. This cured him!

Doc had a new life after I cleaned him up and had his face and back cancer cured. I took care of him and paid all the bills from the beginning. I was not at any time visibly mad; after all, he was family. I gave him an allowance that he really did not need, because I provided everything for him, including a housekeeper/companion, Laura Lee, who was the wife of Willie Cook. She made sure that he bathed every day, put on clean clothes and had three cooked meals. He was on the mend. His previous lifestyle of hording encouraged him to keep the same clothes on for days without bathing. His new routine with Laura Lee ensured that he was clean and presentable.

In 1998, Doc had found another intrigue in the nearest trailer. Every day or two a pair of black panties and bra hung on the clothesline behind his house. Betty and I decided we needed to get him out of the camp for a while before he got himself into trouble again. So, she came to Jensen Beach to see Doc as a surprise for him to travel with her and her husband, Bob, to North Carolina. At first, Doc wasn't too excited about leaving the Camp, but then he warmed to the idea.

Allan's son, Jay, who had come around and was talking to Doc again, provided the first leg of the trip. He took Doc as far as Fort Valley, Georgia.

Doc said, "They have the best peaches in the world."

Jay and his wife, Debbie, stayed the night, had breakfast with them and then headed home. Doc, Betty and Bob continued on to North Carolina.

They had lunch at the Dillard House 30 minutes south of Franklin, North Carolina, where Betty and Bob lived. Doc bought some of their famous country ham and bacon.

The ride from Dillard to Franklin presented a changing canvas of greenery out the car window peppered with views of the Blue Ridge Mountains and filled with lush pastures in the valleys. The native trees adorned the hills and mountains. Here and there, mountain laurel, honeysuckle and rhododendron peeked through the greenery. Doc was speechless with wonder at the transitional beauty. The trip took place the Fourth of July weekend. Summertime is when the native plants flourish and show off their individual dressings. It is quite different from the palm and flowering shrubs of Florida. Doc gazed from side to side taking it all in.

Towering Birch and Hickory trees lined the road through the mountains and provided an umbrella over the car on the snaking roads through one community after another. It felt 10 to 15 degrees cooler in the mountains than in the lower counties.

They finally arrived in Mill Creek in the late afternoon. Betty and Bob's home was a three story wooden structure hanging off the side of the mountain, exposing the grandeur of the forests. The texture of the view ranged from smooth leaves of Magnolias to ruffled leaves of Oak and Maple and finally to prickly needles of Pine and Cedar. Their gated neighborhood provides residents with sufficient space for privacy. After they unloaded the car, they immediately got on the golf cart to give Doc a tour around the community.

Doc said, "This is a perfect place in the mountains."

While he was there, they visited with extended family and old friends. They went to Bridal Veil Falls. They also went to Ruby Mining, the Scottish Tartans Museum and had a picnic lunch beside the Cartoogechaye Creek. At the Chattahoochee

Railroad, an old time mountain band entertained them. To highlight the day, they picked blackberries along the roadside.

They also saw Tallulah Gap.

"I thought I was looking at the Grand Canyon," Doc joked.

He met Minnie Pearl and watched the Dixie Darling Cloggers from Waynesville on this whirlwind visit.

Doc summed up the trip. "Next to Jensen and the Indian River, I like the mountains."

I was happy that I had put things in motion for Doc to get well, feel good, and take a holiday like this. He told Betty, "I appreciate the trip, but Beverly is the only one who ever did anything for me. She took care of my cancer, got me a social security number, hired a housekeeper and provided me with a place to live." Even with this confession, Doc would not share where he had put any of grandmother Pitchford's furniture or furnishings. None of us ever retrieved anything of hers. The greed had hardened his heart and soul to the point he could not feel any love or compassion. He had lost it all. He was a shell of a man and died in 2000 at age 93.

While Doc was gone on the trip with Betty, we rented the Big House to a couple who immediately began cleaning it up and eventually restored the house back to its original beauty. They owned Southern Properties Real Estate. The couple lived upstairs with their office downstairs. They were there many years, but eventually left to build their own place.

That angel was still sitting on my shoulder working out all the details for me to handle these issues.

I also renovated two houses and three apartments on the property where the big house was and rented all of them. This was our land Trust. I sold four acres and a 150-foot waterfront property. I got a contract on Grandfather's Periwinkle house from a foreign group out of Miami called ICE, but the deal fell through because the property only appraised at $500,000 in its current condition. Then a man who owned an RV Park in New Jersey bought it. He didn't need financing, because he had cash from the sale of his New Jersey property. He had big ideas about expanding the campground, building high-rise apartments and a subdivision of small homes on the river.

I needed Lot 6 that Uncle Blount had deeded to Mom and Dad as a wedding present because it was part of the Camp. Dad and Marjorie, Dad's third wife, had moved into Mom and Dad's house in Jensen as they got older and living on a boat became too difficult. After Dad died, Marjorie lived in the house until she died. Marjorie's daughter, Rosemary, also lived in the house with her husband who was a Veteran. Shortly after Marjorie died, Rosemary divorced her husband and moved back to England where she was born and educated. She retained the deed to Lot 6 and the house. I contacted her and she was willing to sell the lot back to me. Therefore, I was in a position to put the Pitchford property together for a sale to one purchaser.

I also got a contract on three apartments and two other houses, including Periwinkle. I sold these properties for $2,000,000.

The years fixing up Pitchford were just plain hard work. I felt like I was going to work every day. There were many crazy things happening along the way. One afternoon I felt the weight of all that we had done and still needed to do. I just couldn't imagine another day of handling all the problems. I told Jack, "I need to get out of this Camp for a while."

Jack was always ready to eat and I guess he realized that I was on the brink of crashing. "Sure. That sounds good. Let's go to dinner at Frank's Fish Shack. We can take the rest of the afternoon off. The drive to Frank's will be a nice change and I can't wait to eat some good seafood."

Jack had learned to be careful when he tried to protect me from working too hard. If he said that I needed to rest or take it easy, I would blow-up and tell him that I could handle it! I guess I always carried a chip on my shoulder that I could do anything that a man could do. My years working with men who disparaged women made me super-sensitive. Therefore, Jack would just make a suggestion of a diversion for me. And it worked!

Frank's Fish Shack was right on the ocean about ten miles out of town. Its name belied the location and structure, which was weathered but sturdy, not a shack. There were brightly colored old metal business signs nailed all over the outside of the restaurant and a 30-foot flashing sign at the road displaying a large fish jumping out of the water identifying its location.

When we drove into the dirt and gravel parking lot, we were unsure if we would find a parking place. There was a long line of patrons waiting to get inside. I was glad to see that the business was doing so well, but disappointed that we would have to wait for a table. The staff was very accommodating and offered to bring us drinks while we waited. We ordered two lemonades and walked over to a rustic bench beside the entrance. Folks were laughing, talking, and not frustrated about waiting for a table. The hostess told us that it would be about 45 minutes before a table would open up.

A clean-cut man in a red plaid shirt got up to let me have a seat, as he tucked his shirt into his jeans, and as I thanked him, he and Jack began talking. The night was clear and a soft breeze lifted the fronds of the palm trees around the restaurant. In the background, we could hear sounds of country music playing. It wasn't loud, but added a nice distraction from thinking too much. I appreciated the music and leaned back to relax and just "be".

I gazed at the water and listened to Jack's conversation with Paul who was from Birmingham, Alabama. He introduced Jack to his wife and his fishing buddy, Dave, and his wife who were from Arkansas. Jack asked them if they were on vacation, and why they came to Jensen Beach.

Paul said, "We come here every year at this time to fish. Dave and I met the first year we both came. During the two weeks we were here, our families had such a good time together that we decided to meet here again the next year. That was 20 years ago and we continue to meet here every year. We've become good friends. We both have motor homes and we park at Pitchfords by the Sea. The pier has great fishing. We go out to eat each night and this is one of our favorite places. The food is always delicious and the folks are friendly and fun. It's not fancy, but we come here to relax."

Jack asked why they camped at Pitchfords when there were other RV Parks in Florida.

Dave spoke up, "I drive from Arkansas and use my vacation days to fish. I do not want to take a chance on going to a place where the fishing is "iffy". Pitchfords has always had great fishing. We know the area and don't have to spend time looking for places to eat or how to get to the water from the RV park. The wives can walk to several places to shop, have lunch or explore. I know that Pitchfords has become run down over the years, but that doesn't bother us. We have our own living quarters, comfortable beds and bathrooms in our RVs. It is a very inexpensive place to park an RV and we save money, because we always stay two weeks."

Paul chimed in, "And we feel safe for our wives. They sometimes bring chairs and sit on the pier for a while, sometimes they fish, but they have the option of doing other things if they choose and the view of the Jensen Bridge is beautiful, especially at night. I've noticed that someone is cleaning up the area this year. It should be back to its old beauty by next year. We loved the feel of the 'old Florida' and look forward to it coming back."

The hostess came out and called their names. Jack shook hands with both men and we told the four of them that we enjoyed meeting them. They would never guess how much they helped me that night. I felt invigorated and after dinner was ready to get back to finishing the job.

The result of the renovation was a fine RV Park of 114 units with a beautiful office up front decorated with antique furniture and photos from the big house, Periwinkle, which hosted Christmas Parties and other big events.

Our last year's gross was almost $500,000. I had opened a clean, well-designed laundry there that netted about $10,000 a year. We also had the restaurant across the street on the Indian River. I sold the Park for $6,500,000, and divided it among the four direct heirs and earlier had sold the Periwinkle property at just the right time for $2,000,000. I divided the $2,000,000 12 ways: the four heirs (all had two children) eight grandchildren. I felt good to make all 12 remaining descendants happy.

My job was finished. I had taken all of the Pitchford properties and restored them back to their glory days. Selling my family's dynasty was sad but fulfilling, because it could have remained rundown and continued to deteriorate and eventually be worth nothing.

I hoped that my work ethic learned from my dad, and love of my heritage finally crushed the Pitchford curse. I proved that you can't just sit back and accumulate wealth. You have to work it, manage it and love the job in order to have more than you started with.

CHAPTER 27

Life in the Military Community

While living in Jensen, we built a house in the west end of the camp. We had something like $300,000 in it. Jack was the overseer of our house. When we put it on the market the buyer asked us what we wanted for it, Jack was about to say $400,000. I spoke up and said $550,000. Thankfully, it sold for $550,000.

We moved on to Melbourne, Florida.

2004 (age 77)

We were so blessed to live in Melbourne. We had the best of everything at the Indian River Colony Club. We loved our next five years. It was like every other event in my life. I never planned on living in a place like this. As a young person, I never sat around dreaming of what I would be when I grew up. I didn't let things that happened frazzle me. I never moaned over what I didn't have, or question what I had been given. I just lived for each day, took each issue as a challenge, and made the best of it.

God blessed me with a life that was challenging, fulfilling, exciting and fruitful. I thank Him for that. I knew he was putting me in the places I should be and guiding me on how to function in those places. It was especially easy now.

We had a beautifully redecorated home on water near the golf course with miles of green carpet turf. The house could host over 40 guests at a time for parties. The community was for Retired Military officers only, but beyond that initial criteria, no one could pull rank. We were all equal. Many generals lived there, but their rank meant nothing. There was an eighteen-hole golf course, a beautiful club and restaurant. The clubhouse had a three-story glass front facing the golf course. It was natural rock on the other three sides, which were fifty percent glass. There was a large pool, carpeted workout area and a ballroom that could accommodate 500 people. The kitchen was large enough to cook for banquets and monthly parties. There was also a high-end restaurant located on the main floor.

Once again, we enjoyed a full social life. It was like being back in the Air Force. We had many opportunities to "dress up" too. There were opportunities for me to wear some of the formal outfits I had purchased when I sold real estate and attended many events in Washington, DC and Virginia.

Then, Jack began falling and spent several days in the hospital after each fall. He had a caregiver at home in Indian River Country Club for a while. At that point, the doctor told us we needed to move closer to family because things would not get better. We found a home in a 55-and-older community in Georgia, near our daughter Jacque.

Our son-in-law, Bill, flew down and drove us back and forth from Georgia to Melbourne, FL for several years, but we finally realized that we needed to sell. Bill rented a U-Haul and took some of our possessions to a warehouse near our new home. Then he flew back to Melbourne to drive us to Georgia for the final time.

On the last drive from Florida to Georgia, we passed through many small towns. I looked out the window at many abandoned towns and wondered why people stopped loving these places. Houses and businesses covered in dust, with hollow spaces that should have windowpanes, looked like the soul of the house left. I realized that these towns, without love and caring, attention and maintenance died from within. Homes, businesses, towns and people need constant nurturing. When they don't get it, the soul eventually leaves and it becomes a shallow shell. The trip brought back sad memories of my life for many reasons.

CHAPTER 28

Jack's Illness

About 2010 (age 83)

We had a condominium in Mill Creek Country Club, Franklin, NC for several years. When we bought the villa in Georgia, we brought some furniture from the Mill Creek condo to furnish it. Jacque's husband, Bill, moved the furniture with their new horse trailer.

We did go back and forth to Mill Creek for a couple of years, even though Jack was sick. Bill flew down and drove us back to Franklin several times over the years. On our last trip from Franklin, we took some more precious things to our new home. We sold the Mill Creek Condo.

Selling our beautiful home in Melbourne was a different situation. There were strict rules about selling personal belongings in that restricted neighborhood, so we left almost everything for the association sales manager to sell. She was in charge of selling home contents. A homeowners' restriction required that anything sold in the community had to go through her. We expected her to be fair with pricing our furniture and fixtures. She was not. She was in complete control of what sold, to whom and for how much. She practically gave away very expensive pieces of furniture for very little money and donated far too much to the local charity. We received pennies on the dollar for all of our contents.

We never got a reconciliation of any transaction. We just got a check for about one fourth of what we left in the house and what did sell was pennies on the dollar. The remainder of our good furniture was "donated". We had no control and no desire, at this time in our life, to fight for what was rightfully ours.

Through all the changes in our life, through good times and bad times, our love remained strong. We were not a mushy-mushy couple. We kept our love private, but Jack could send the sweetest cards. On my 86th birthday on December 17, 2013, Jack gave me a lavender butterfly card with the verse:

"For My Wife

In the whirlwind of our lives, with each day flying into the next, It seems easy to take our love for granted, to forget what life was like Before we had each other...

But whenever I slow down a little, and just look into your eyes, I still feel that spark of fire that first brought us close, I still Hear the whisper in my heart that first told me we were made For each other...

So I want you to know, on your birthday and always, I treasure our love and you.

Happy Birthday

(Beverly. This card truly expresses my feelings and Love I have For you.)

Jack"

2015 (age 88)

Jack passed away June 27, 2015. My last words to him were, "I'm here. We're at Dades Drug Store."

The family later said I was trying to bring him back. All the family was around his bed on the second floor of intensive care. At the end he opened his eyes, stared wide-eyed upwards and we are sure he saw the light of Heaven.

Jack is already in Heaven and I plan to join him one day. We have a resting place in the Military Section of our local cemetery.

Some nights I can feel Jack's breath on my shoulder when I'm snuggled in bed. I'll move over to his side of the bed and feel the warmth from his body. Then I will look at his picture across the room and he will wink at me. I am at peace at that moment.

He is waiting for me. He is the other half of my spirit. Our years together were not perfect all the time, but they were filled with magic, adventure and our drives for each of our professions, and love and respect for each other and each other's needs. We had seventy years of living life our way.

Death leaves a heartache no one can heal.
Love leaves a memory no one can steal. *
*(Quoted from an Irish
Headstone by Richard Puz)

EPILOGUE

Since Jack's death, I spend much of my day on the computer. I shop and look up clothing deals at Chico's and read news stories. One day I was bored with this activity, so I decided to look up the Pitchford property in Jensen Beach.

I was startled to see articles in the local paper about citizens challenging the rezoning applications at the County Commission meetings in Jensen Beach. The purchaser of the Pitchford Campground property had proposed two multi-story apartment and condominium buildings on the Indian River with single-family homes on the majority of the rest of the land. Nevertheless, the community fought his re-zoning efforts for years. He finally gave up on making the Pitchford, Ltd. a mega development, and then gave up on maintaining the property.

Looking at reviews of the property in its current state broke my heart. The pictures and reviews revealed a look back in time before I restored the property. Because the owner could not get permission to develop the property where he could make a profit, he just let it sit with no improvements and no maintenance. It looked worse than I remembered it back in 1994.

A haunting thought crossed my mind. Maybe there was more to the 'curse' than just the Pitchford family. Maybe the property had the curse. Either way, I never intend to look at the current pictures again or talk with anyone about the property's condition. I will let that curse lie.